MW01182246

LOVE LOST, LOVE GAINED

LOVE LOST, LOVE GAINED

by
Claire M. Ford

Pittsburgh, PA

ISBN 1-58501-020-0

Paperback fiction
© Copyright 2000 Claire M. Ford
All rights reserved
First Printing—2000
Library of Congress #99-65238

Request for information should be addressed to:

CeShore Publishing Co.
The Sterling Building
440 Friday Road
Pittsburgh, PA 15209
www.ceshore.com

Cover design: Michelle S. Vennare - SterlingHouse Publisher
Typesetting: McBeth Typesetting and Design
CeShore Publishing Company is an imprint of SterlingHouse Publisher, Inc.

This is a work of fiction. Names, characters, incidents, and places, are the
product of the author's imagination or are used fictitiously.
Any resemblance to actual events or persons, living or dead
is entirely coincidental.

Printed in Canada

DEDICATION

I would like to dedicate this book to my mother,
Ethel Ford and my sister, Cathy Ford. Without their
encouragement and support this endeavor would
not have become a reality.

Chapter One

Maggie could not be happier. Riding along, looking out at the falling snow and dark clouds, she could only sit back with a sigh of contentment and smile. How long she had waited for this day!

Any hopes she once had of her dreams ever coming true had vanished a long time ago. Until today actually happened, she wondered if it really would be more than a life-long fantasy. But it did happen. Today she had gotten married and was now riding to New York with the most handsome and loving man she had ever met. Even in her dreams, Maggie could not have pictured such a creature.

Squeezing his hand, she looked again at Jeff, her husband of, oh, seven hours now. He squeezed her hand in response and smiled down at her and her heart jumped a beat, as it did the first day she laid eyes on him almost two years ago. Mrs. Margaret Reyfield would never forget that day as long as she lived.

May 12, 1991 had finally arrived. Maggie Stelson, a senior at Boston University, was putting the finishing touches on her last paper of her college career.

"There she beamed "Nothing to do now but drop this baby by Dr. Roberts' office.

She could, of course, put it in the box of inter-campus mail, but it was such a beautiful day and Mags felt as though she had been cooped up in this room for a thousand years. Besides, she had been struggling with this masterpiece for weeks and couldn't risk losing it now. All she needed was for it to get lost on route to her professor. Just last week one of her friends had placed her written exam in "i-c" and it had never made it to the destination . Now poor Terry was in the process of writing the thing all over again. Maggie was determined this would not happen to her. Looking out her apartment window she could see the beautiful blue sky and the budding trees in Boston Commons. They were beckoning to her, and her cramped legs were crying out for exercise. She had to go.

Rose, her long time friend and roommate, had left at eight for her last exam. It was an oral and she was a wreck worrying about it. Maggie had just laughed at her friend who was about to graduate summa cum laude. She had listened to Rose's descriptions of the different philosophers and their theories until she could almost repeat them and knew her friend would do exceptionally well - she always did. They had made plans to meet at the Student Union at noon and have lunch together. Both would be graduating the following Friday and felt a celebration was warranted when they finished their work. After lunch they planned to go into downtown Boston to Filene's or Jordan Marsh and indulge themselves with new outfits. Rose laughed on her way out earlier, "Who knows? We may even feel the urge to tackle Filene's basement."

Maggie just rolled her eyes at that and went back to her paper. Filene's basement was THE bargain basement in the state and it was a literal zoo. You almost had to take out life insurance before going there. People grab, push, shove and even yank things out of your hands if you're not alert. It took talent to be a basement shopper. Maggie often thought they should offer courses in the art. She laughed as she thought of a title: "Basement Shopping 101."

"Enough you," she reprimanded herself. "You have work to do." She walked over to the tiny kitchenette on the other side of the room, grabbed a Pepsi and got back to her editing.

She and Rose had been lucky to find this studio apartment so close to campus and with a great view of the park. They had stayed in the dorm their first two years and hated it. Both of them were too serious about their studies to find all the parties and pranks any fun. The duo had talked about getting their own "pad", as Rose called it, but that's all it was: talk, until Rose missed one of her finals and Maggie her last linguistics class because some idiot wedged pennies between the door and frame, making it impossible to open the door. It was only when one of Rose's classmates had missed her that they were found. Rose pleaded with her professor until she was finally allowed to make up the exam, but Rose was so angry she didn't do as well as she could have. Maggie was relieved to find out that the last class was more of a social and she didn't miss anything. Still, their idle talk quickly changed to serious research after that and both agreed to keep eyes and ears open.

Ray, a nickname Rose picked up at school because she often signed notes with only her initials, R.A., happened to be out jogging one Sunday when she noted a sign "FOR RENT" in the window of an old brownstone on Maple Street just off Commonwealth Avenue. It was a nice, well- kept building from the outside, with rose bushes just beginning to bud and a small but neatly trimmed front lawn. Most of the buildings in this area were right on the sidewalk, due to their age. They were built before the roads and sidewalks were ever considered, so even a tiny yard seemed a luxury.

On impulse, Rose sought out the owner and checked the apartment out. She fell in love with it immediately and knew Mags would love it also. The view alone would probably convince her friend. For as long as Rose knew her, Maggie had an almost abnormal need to be able to see outside or what was coming. They often laughed when they'd go out to eat and Maggie always grabbed the seat that had a view of everything.

Rose accepted this "quirk" in her best friend and knew a view and "space" would be Mags' first priority.

After running all the way home, Rose burst into the dorm room in such a way that all Maggie could think was, "Hurricane Rose". As she bent over to pick up the letter she had been writing, which managed to go flying when she was so startled by her friend's boisterous entry, Mags wondered if Rose had finally lost it completely.

3

"I found it she blurted. "The perfect place for us to park our-selves for the remainder of our college days!" "Here," she tossed Maggie her coat. "Let's go."

" I can't go anywhere;I have a class in twenty minutes. Besides, I'm not sure I understand you. Found what? You're talking so fast. Why don't you start again?"

Rose was always the impetuous one of the pair while Maggie was very reserved and had to have every detail before making any decisions. The two seemed to compliment each other over the years. Maybe that's why they had been inseparable since third grade .

Between gasps, Rose delivered her exciting news.

"I've found the most beautiful apartment for us. It's only a stu-dio, but it's clean and furnished. It's on the third floor of a lovely old brownstone and has a great view of the Commons. It's big and roomy and, best of all, it's in our price range. Mr. Coolidge, the owner, claims it will go fast but he will give us first chance at it. Please come see it!"

"You've already seen it! You went upstairs, alone with a man you didn't know! What if this man were a rapist or something? How could you go into a building with him alone?"

"You're crazy, you know that?" Ray glared at her friend. " As long as I've known you, you've worried too much. Stop being your mother for once and come with me. Besides, it is right on the way to your class, the class you are going to be late for anyway!"

" Oh, no!" Maggie yelled. They had been arguing for a good fif-teen minutes. *Oh well*, she thought. *I hate it here. Rose is sponta-neous, but has good instincts about things. By the time I get to class it will be too late, so why not go along?*

To her friend's amazement, Maggie flung her books onto the bed along with her unfinished letter, grabbed her coat, exclaimed, "What the hell- let's go," and headed for the door. After picking her chin up off the floor, Ray ran to catch up to her roommate and gave her all the details as they hurried back to Maple Street.

Maggie loved the spacious flat as soon as she saw it. It was one large room with a small bathroom connected. A quick scan from the doorway told Ray's friend there would be plenty of space for both of

4

them. To her right was a small kitchenette with an apartment-sized stove. It had a large, mustard colored refrigerator in the corner.

What an awful color, she thought, but kept her eyes moving. There were a few cabinets over a sink and minimal counter space; however, she was sure it was plenty for them.

Near the kitchen area was a small, formica-topped table with three matching chairs. "The fourth," explained Mr. Coolidge, "is having the seat repaired. I will have it back here by the end of the week. These vinyl seats tear quite easily."

Across the room from the dining area was a large over-stuffed couch which they were told can pull out into a bed, a matching chair with non-matching footstool, a small end table on the left of the couch and old coffee table in front. There was also a small desk and chair in the far corner with a hanging lamp above it. There was a light on the end table as well as an overhead light with ceiling fan attached. Directly opposite the door were three large windows side by side almost creating a wall in themselves. A built-in window seat invited anyone in the room to sit and enjoy the view. To the right of the windows was a daybed with a small bureau beside it. Maggie immediately walked across the solid wood floor which had a worn braided rug that she guessed to be about eight feet by ten feet. After looking out, then turning and again scanning the room from that angle, Mags grinned at Ray and cried, "I love it! It needs some of your creativity to 'cozy it up', if you know what I mean. But it has character and charm, and the view is totally awesome." Turning to Mr. Coolidge, who claimed to be a distant relative of the past president, she questioned, "So, when can we move in?"

"You can sign the papers tomorrow and the place is yours," responded the kind, elderly gentleman with a sparsely-toothed grin.

"I'm glad you'll be taking it," he continued. When I suggested to my wife that we rent it to college students, she was afraid of loud parties and drugs and stuff. The two of you don't look like that type and she'll be pleased. Tomorrow, when you come to sign the lease, you can meet her. She'll love you two, I'm sure."

"Mrs. Coolidge is a doll," exclaimed Rose, as she and Maggie left the building with lease in hand the following afternoon.

"I liked her at once", replied Mags. Then throwing her arms around her friend and hugging her, Maggie added, "Ray, I am so glad you found this place. I just know it will be great."

Three days later they began moving their belongings into their new apartment

With a sudden start, Maggie realized she had been daydreaming again. Mags grabbed her sweater and paper, locked the front door and began her last trip along the route she knew so well. Mr. Roberts, known to his students as Dan, would only be there for another half hour. If she didn't get a move on she'd never make it and would have to subject her paper to "i-c". That thought alone caused her to move faster.

Practically running, Maggie arrived at the education building with time to spare. She caught Dan who was gathering up his things and talking on the phone at the same time, and with a grin handed him her latest work.

"Thanks, Margaret," said Dan, as he placed the receiver in its place. "I knew you would be by today. You are the most punctual of all my students."

Dan was able to hear, but spent so much time with the Deaf community that he was considered Deaf by all who knew him. Therefore, time had no relevance for him and deadlines were not carved in stone. As long as papers and take-homes were handed in before the next semester began he didn't worry about such things as deadlines and time limits a typical Deaf mentality. *At least*, Maggie thought, *in the Boston area.*

Her major was Deaf Education. Thus she associated a great deal with Deaf people and attended many Deaf functions and none was begun on time. She and her classmates knew if the professor was Deaf the class began fifteen minutes later than scheduled. There was no real explanation for it. It was just a given: Deaf people were always late! Although, Maggie accepted this, she herself could not be tardy. There was something in her that drove her to be on time, if not early.

"You're welcome, Dan," Mags responded to her professor, advisor and mentor. "See you at graduation. Now that I'm free I am going to stroll through Boston Commons and enjoy the day."

Maggie practically skipped out of the office and around the corner heading to the Commons. A feeling of lightness had engulfed her and she just wanted to get away from campus and become absorbed in nature. The trees were gorgeous and the robins' chirping told her they were making themselves known again after winter. Winter had been long and furious this year, surprising everyone by dumping six inches of snow just four weeks ago. *But you'd never know that now*, she thought, looking up at the clear, blue sky. It seemed to sparkle at Maggie and congratulate her for completing her work. She noted one lone cloud up above and thought, giggling, that it looked like a puffy, white shoe. Then all of a sudden she went down.

Next thing she knew, she was on the ground rubbing her foot, trying to figure out what happened. Then she realized: She had tripped over a tree root while dreaming, and lost her balance.

What a klutz she thought. *I can't believe I did that. I better stop trying to analyze clouds and pay attention.* She smiled at the thought of calling Rose and saying, "I can't meet you for lunch. Why? I was looking at a giant, white, shoe in the sky, tripped and broke my leg." However, after feeling her ankle, she breathed a sigh of relief: It was just bruised.

Still smiling, Maggie looked up and her heart began beating so hard she thought the world could hear it. There, staring down at her, was the most beautiful man she had ever seen. He was holding out his hand to help her up but she was too stunned to take it. All she wanted to do was sit and stare at his beautiful face.

She was looking at a rugged but gentle face with the bluest eyes she had ever seen. He must have been about six feet, she figured, with a body so sleek and muscular that he had to be an athlete, or else live at the gym. There was not one ounce of fat anywhere on his gorgeous body. He had inky black hair and carefully trimmed

7

beard and a small scar over his left eye. His nose was a little crooked but fit his face like a glove. Maggie - quiet, calculating Maggie - was in love.

After what seemed like an eternity, she reached up and took his hand and he pulled her up. She felt his strength and standing near him she could smell the Brute he was wearing and almost melted in his arms.

She was right: he was over six feet and they seemed to fit together like they were made for each other.

"Thank you," she stammered. "I can't believe I did that. I guess I will always be clumsy. My mother always told me I daydreamed too much and never watched what I was doing."

Realizing she was rambling, Maggie bit her lip and began to blush.

What is wrong with me? she thought. *He must think I'm a real geek.*

Jeffrey Michael Reyfield only smiled at her and pointed to his ears, shaking his head. He then started walking in the direction of the swan boats. Margaret watched him stroll out of her life forever, until it hit her that that's what would happen. She didn't even know his name. All she knew about him was he was Deaf and incredibly gorgeous

You fool, she thought, *Go after him. You have been too cautious in your life and missed out on so much. Don't lose him now.*

Maggie startled herself by running after him, getting his attention and signing to him, "My name is Margaret Stelson. Thank you for helping me. I was just going to have lunch. Want to join me?" Rose had vanished from her mind completely.

Jeff looked into her deep brown eyes and smiled. "Okay", he signed. " I know a great place.

I was just on my way there. Can I take you?"

She nodded, suddenly aware of her brashness and blushing slightly. If he noticed her sudden redness, he said nothing. He simply smiled at her, grabbed her hand and started toward the subway station. Maggie was actually finding it difficult to keep up, an experience completely new for her.

Maggie was six feet tall herself and most of her height was in her legs. She had long brown hair and deep brown eyes. She was a pretty girl with a nice figure, but never thought of herself as attractive. Her mother was always telling her, "You seem to be gaining weight"or "Why don't you lighten you hair to bring out your eyes?" and so on.

The kids at school always teased her for being the tallest one in the class. At age ten she was already five feet tall. She dreaded anything that required the class to line up according to height.

"Leggie Maggie goes to the end", they would chant. "Mags, Mags with the big long legs."

Even her best friend Rose Arlton could not help her as she was always close to the front of the line. People always referred to them as Mutt and Jeff.

The subway was very crowded so Maggie and Jeff were pushed together. Trying to hold the pole and keep from falling, Maggie realized the dilemma she faced: How could she talk to Jeff?

He had no problem and did most of the small talk until they reached their stop.

She was a little taken aback and hesitant when he took her to a very small, dingy storefront in Harvard Square. She had never done anything like this in her life and began to have second thoughts. The place looked like a real dive from the outside, yet something told her not to back out now. She could just imagine Rose's reaction later: "Girl, you are crazy! It's about time!"

Holding the door for her, he escorted her into the tiny, building and to her surprise it turned out to be a quaint and gorgeous little café which was soon to become their special place.

Mags could not believe what she saw. It was cozy, and clean, with about ten small tables. Each table had a pale blue tablecloth with an orange scented candle in the center. Pictures on the wall showed different scenes of Harvard Square and University life. Some were purchased at the Coupe, Harvard University's famous book store, but many were enlarged photographs taken by the owner himself. Jeff pointed out some of the nuances to her while they waited for their waitress. Maggie watched his hands and lovingly took in the beauty of her surroundings at the same time. It had a charming ambiance which made her feel welcome and comfortable. The cafe was enchanting, and Mags made a mental note to bring Rose some day soon.

Shortly after ordering, Maggie saw Jeff's eyes look beyond her and he smiled. She looked around to see a young man in a white apron approach the table and welcome Jeff. The man, whom she assumed was the cook, signed fluently with Jeff, and Mags tried desperately to keep up with the conversation. Later it was explained to her that the man was Jeff's older brother and he too was deaf. He had graduated five years ago from Harvard and owned the restaurant.

"Dave struggled to get his degree in business management and always wanted to own a restaurant," Jeff explained "He has always loved to cook and is wonderful at his art. He's saving his money and is hoping to move to a larger building by next year. He came upon this place quite by accident. It was very run down and needed quite a bit of work. Because of this, Dave got the place for a real bargain, then conned the whole family into helping fix it up. I guess you can say I am part owner of this establishment."

While waiting for their food, Jeff explained that he had two brothers and one sister. Dave and himself were the only two children who were Deaf. Their parents were also Deaf. Their dad was a machinist in a shoe factory until he took early retirement last year. He worked extremely hard and wanted the very best for his children. Jeff's mom had been sickly for as long as he'd known her so Dave learned early how to cook and care for his brothers and sister. Jeff idolized his brother who was seven years his senior. After Dave there was Anna, now twenty - six, who was a teacher in Chicago. She was married and had an eight month old son. Then Jeff came along and when he was four his brother Paul was born. Paul is graduating from high school in a month. Jeff's family lived in a small town north of Boston called Beverly.

The food arrived then and was wonderful and quite filling. Until she took the first bite, Maggie hadn't realized how hungry she really was. She was glad she had ordered a sandwich instead of the quiche. The latter would have grown cold while she tried to absorb all Jeff was telling her. He finished long before her, even though he was doing all the signing. It always amazed her how Deaf people could sign and eat at the same time. She savored every word and could not stop looking at him.

The afternoon passed much too quickly. After saying goodbye to Dave, they left the restaurant and strolled back to the subway. By now it was about three o'clock. He showed her different little shops which she had never seen before and pointed out some of the history of the area. She longed for the afternoon to never end, but all too soon they arrived at her building. Jeff pecked her lightly on the cheek and promised to call her again. She floated up the stairs to her room.

"Where have you been?", yelled Rose, when Mags opened the door. "We were going to meet for lunch after you delivered your 'masterpiece,' remember? By the way, did your title fit on the paper? My exam went okay and I was looking forward to celebrating. When you didn't show I came home and ate the leftover chicken. What did happen, anyway?"

When Maggie didn't answer, Rose turned around and saw her leaning on the wall and immediately recognized "the look."

"Okay, who is he?" she asked. Mags' grin covered her whole face as tears of joy ran down her cheeks. She looked at Ray, who was awed beyond words, and started talking. After her first words, Rose knew her friend was not going to be single for much longer, and on February 27, 1993, as the maid of honor , she watched as her long-time friend became Mrs. Margaret JoAnn Reyfield and tears dripped into the bouquet she was holding. Rose knew her friend better than anyone in the church and prayed that this marriage would bring her the true love and happiness she always longed for.

Later, at the reception, David Reyfield, the best man, stood to toast the young newlyweds. As he signed and the interpreter voiced for him, two seats at the table remained empty. Maggie's parents did not attend her wedding.

Jeff was shaking her awake, now. He had pulled into a small diner and asked if she was hungry. Her hands said yes while in her mind she was saying, *Please, Mom, it wasn't my fault.*

Chapter Two

22 Years Earlier

"Jake, it's time. Jake hurry!"

Molly Stelson stood at the bottom of the stairs, calling to her husband of four years. She had been baking a cake for their anniversary celebration when the pains began. Turning off the oven, she waddled uncomfortably into the living room, knowing this time it was real. Her babies were coming.

Now two weeks overdue, Molly had rushed to the hospital three different times only to be sent back home after being told they were false alarms.

She had made the comment that people would think she was crying wolf next time, but the nurse assured her this was common, especially for first-time mothers.

Though this would be her first delivery, Molly had been pregnant twice before and had had two miscarriages. Her doctor had been watching her very carefully this time. He was truly pleased with her progress. Molly took every precaution and followed his instructions, sometimes to an extreme. She even took the last two months off from work to assure the babies' safety. Pat, her boss, was not thrilled, but understood the fears and let her go, but not without managing to get Molly's promise of a quick return. "After all, you've become invaluable around here. How can I survive without you?"

Molly was an assistant to Patty Walsch, a famous caterer in Buffalo, New York. Her job was to set up parties, plan menus, and the like. She came in contact with some very important people, and was always getting referrals, and bringing in new business. She loved her job, and it showed in the pleasant way she treated her customers. Pat was always appreciative of her work and over the years the two had become close friends, even though many times Pat tried to mother her. Pat was even considering making Molly a full-time partner. Therefore, when Molly left her office Ms. Patricia Walsch felt as if her right arm had been severed.

"Good luck, Molly. I hope all will be okay." She had seen what Molly and Jake had been through in the past and she ached for her young friends.

Now, two and a half months later, all Molly could think about was the pain and the urgency of getting to the hospital.

Jake, whose full name was James Ronald Stelson, III, came down the stairs, taking them two at a time. Within minutes, he had the car out front and was helping Molly into the front seat.

It was a beautiful day, sunny and delightfully warm. They kept the windows rolled down as they sped to the hospital five miles away. At this point, Jake could drive the route in his sleep, but stared out the window in what appeared to be a wide-eyed stupor. He knew how devastated Molly had been over the loss of the other two babies, and he didn't want to do anything foolish, like get into an accident. All he wanted was to get her to the delivery room safely.

Following her second miscarriage, she stayed in her bed for two full weeks and would see no one. Then, as if nothing happened, she was her old self again. She told Jake she had had a dream that she had given birth to twins and they were screaming for her, so she had to get up. Throughout this third pregnancy, she remained convinced she was having twins, even though her doctor was quite sure there was only one.

Arriving at the emergency room, Jake prayed that this time the baby would be healthy, for both Molly's sake, and his. She had been so distant lately he was afraid he was losing her.

Maybe the child will be the bond we need, he thought.

Labor lasted eight hours and Molly was becoming exhausted. The doctor kept offering her some medication, but she insisted that she wanted to stay alert.

"I must see my babies when they come," she said. "I want to be the first to hold them and tell them I love them."

Jake hoped she wouldn't be too disappointed when there was only one baby. He had finally convinced her, after many discussions, to set up only one nursery. They could always buy seconds of things later, if needed. "*When* needed!" she instantly corrected him.

As Jake reached down to wipe her forehead, a shrill cry filled the room. Leaning over to show Molly her child, the doctor announced, "It's a girl. She's beautiful!"

"Doctor!" the nurse's voice sounded troubled. "Look!"

Then he spotted her. A tiny little girl laid still in the womb. She was not moving, and he had to reach in and pull her out. It appeared she had died during the second trimester, as she was not completely formed. How could he tell Molly about this second child? He knew better than anyone how much she had suffered at the loss of her previous two babies. He also knew her mental state was vulnerable at this point. Jake had confided in him, and Molly had told him a number of times about her dream. Only last week he'd noted a mass on the ultrasound, and feared the worst. Now those fears had been realized, and he would have to say something. He was not sure how to voice his findings, and remained quiet until Molly's weak voice brought him back to reality.

"We'll name this one Margaret and the other one Patricia," said Molly. "Where is the other one, Doctor? I know there are two. Has she come yet?"

When she didn't hear any screams, Molly began to yell, "What's wrong? Where's my baby?"

"Molly, Jake there is another little girl but she is stillborn," the doctor spoke quietly and gently. "It appears she died about five months after conception. I'm very sorry." His heart ached for them and he could feel a tear roll down his cheek.

Molly cried as if her world was ending, and clung to little Margaret. The nurses had to pry the baby loose to get her cleaned up. From that day on, little Maggie became her mother's obsession - or was it Patty?

Jake cringed when he heard the doctor's words. How could this happen again? As he listened to his wife's sobbing, he knew their life together would never be the same. He had so hoped that this would be a new start for them both.

Four years ago it was all so different, he remembered.

"Here she comes," whispered Don, his long time friend and best man.

Turning to look, Jake's eyes met Molly's and suddenly no one else was important, or even present. In her beautiful white dress, Molly resembled an angel, and her beautiful smile made all his nervous doubts disappear. When they pronounced their vows and promised to cherish each other always, he believed he was in heaven. Then, at the end of the ceremony when he lifted her veil to give her a kiss, she was grinning so much her whole face glowed and he knew he loved her even more than he thought possible.

That first year of marriage, there was pure joy and love. Molly's energy and zest for life rubbed off, and he began to enjoy being alive in a way he never had before. She showed him things about himself that he never knew were there. He began to love operas, plays, museums, and other cultural arts that before were torture for him. Molly loved these things, and could explain them all to him in a way that made him ask for more.

As a youth he was exposed to these cultural events, finding them boring and endless. He had countless fights with his parents when he refused to go with them. But not with Molly. With her, every day was a new adventure in learning. He actually longed for their outings. Even when he had to wear a tie, he felt free and alive.

Jake remembered the time he and Molly went to New York City for the weekend. Saturday was to be spent at the art museum. He had her in stitches telling her of his earliest memory of the Metropolitan.

"I believe I was seven then and my sisters were ten and twelve. They came running up to me when I got home from playing to tell me the 'good news.' The news was that my mother was taking us into the city the next day. We would take the train, and go to the art museum to see an exhibit by a famous painter named Picasso.

"I couldn't even pronounce his name and couldn't understand why they wouldn't let me stay home. I asked Mom if I could go to Donny's house or something. Heck, I pleaded, but she would not hear of it. Mom felt that the exposure to culture will be good for me. She assured me that I'd love it when I saw it.

"Of course, I ended up going and thought of my dad throughout the long train ride. He had to work on some papers and couldn't go with us. How I envied him! I thought the pictures were the weirdest things and spent more time playing with my tie and getting drinks from every bubbler we came to. I couldn't understand how everyone could just stand and admire painting after painting. I thought they were the ugliest things I ever saw.

"When we got home, mom told dad she would never take me again until I was 'much older.' I hooped and hollered all the way up the stairs. Later I learned she had told dad that all I did was whine, complain and interrupt her to take me to the bathroom."

He went on to explain that he believed he hated the "cultural stuff" because no one ever tried to teach him about anything. Now Molly was showing him all the richness of culture that he had missed as a child. As he learned, he understood the beauty of fine art, music, and drama. Now he knew the answer to the "why?"

"It's an expectation of high - class society," his parents had told him. Now, with his beautiful wife, it was just pure fun.

Growing up, there were times he hated being rich. He often wished he could live a simple, quiet life where he didn't have to put on a show for people, go to boring parties, and take piano lessons. He loved his parents, but sometimes they could be out and out snobs. His two older sisters thrived on the grandeur of wealth and were often embarrassed when he preferred playing stickball in the "poor" section of town. He did all he could in school to hide his wealth and be "like the other kids" who in many ways seemed happier than he. He vividly remembered the day he overslept, missing the bus and had to get a ride to school. He begged his mother to take him in her car but, no - she had William drive him. He rode up to the front door in a shiny limo. He spotted all the kids hanging out the classroom windows. They jeered when his chauffeur opened the door for him. He died of embarrassment that day. From then on he never overslept again.

Molly's simple, child-like love of life carried over in all she did and he adored her for it. In mid- September when she found out she was pregnant, he was ecstatic. He took her to the fanciest restaurant he could find to celebrate. They toasted the baby and the life that would come from their love together. They were so excited and so in love. Life just couldn't be better.

Her first two months were hard. She was sick every morning, and Jake found he was running out many nights buying her whatever she craved. Her favorite seemed to be pistachio ice cream, of all things. By the end of October she seemed to be feeling better, and her morning sickness came to an end.

Molly's parents had invited them for Thanksgiving and since she was still weak Molly was glad to go. The day was chaotic since two of Molly's four brothers, along with their wives and children, arrived for the festivities. Not present were Bob who was overseas working for an oil firm in Spain, and Phillip was sick. Molly's dad could never forgive Phil and she knew he would not be welcome, so she assumed "sick" was an excuse rather than a fact.

Despite the confusion, both Molly and Jake were sorry to see the day's end. They received many hugs and kisses as they retrieved their coats from the spare room. Jake noted it was seven o'clock when they reluctantly backed out the driveway.

"I thoroughly enjoy your family," Jake laughed. "They do know how to celebrate! I think they're hoping we will provide them with their first granddaughter. Shall we oblige? What do you think?"

Receiving no answer, he looked over and his smile broadened. Molly had fallen asleep with a peaceful grin on her radiant face.

Jake had to swerve quickly to avoid an oncoming car, and decided he had better watch the road instead of looking at his beautiful wife. As he swerved , Molly suddenly shrieked.

"Oh my God, what happened?" she wailed.

"Nothing, sweetheart - that car just got a little too close. I'm sorry I woke you. Go back to sleep."

All of a sudden she shrieked again, and this time when Jake looked, she was doubled over in pain. She was wearing a look of sheer torture on her face.

Without hesitation, Jake sped to the nearby hospital and Molly awoke hours later to Jake's sad eyes.

"Where am I?" she asked when she saw her husband.

"You're in the hospital. You were quite sick, and very weak, but the doctor says you'll be fine."

Feeling her flat stomach, she whispered weakly, "Where is my baby?"

"The doctor says we can always have more. You are still young. You need to rest now and get your strength back."

"No, I don't want to rest. I want my baby," she sobbed. "Don't hide her from me."

"Molly, you had a miscarriage. You lost the baby. The doctor said this often happens with the first pregnancy and the important thing is you need to get your health back. I promise you we will have another baby."

The sparkle in Molly's eyes was gone; all she could do was shake her head and sob. It seemed like hours that he simply held her and rocked her when the nurse came in and told him he had to leave.

A week later, Molly came home. She was physically well again, but a part of her had died with the baby. She could still laugh and have fun with him, but that buoyancy and sparkle he loved in her were gone. There was a place inside of her that he could not reach no matter how he tried. He ached for her and prayed daily for his old Molly to return to him.

Finally, in early fall, 1968, she was pregnant again. She told him she was thrilled, but she was also scared and overly cautious.

She withdrew to her bed, only getting up for meals or to sit in the living room and watch TV.

"I'm doing it to protect my baby," she'd say when he tried to get her to go out with him. "If you cared about my baby, you'd understand."

"It's my baby too and I do care," he argued.

"You're not helping him or you this way. The doctor says exercise and fresh air will do you good."

There was no convincing her, so Jake left her alone. He loved her so much and felt so helpless.

Two months later she called to him in the night and said, "My baby's gone." He saw the blood- stained sheets and knew what had happened. Filled with foreboding, he gently lifted her in his arms and carried her downstairs. By the time they arrived at the hospital she had passed out. The next time he saw her, she was all cleaned up and looked as lovely as ever, but there was a deep sadness in her eyes and she appeared to be in a trance.

When he took her home a few days later, she immediately went to bed and stayed in the dark room for the next two weeks. He tried to talk to her but she had shut him out. He could only bring her food, which she ate very little of, and pray. He slept in the guest room because she wouldn't even let him in her bed.

Just when he was about to give in to the advice of family and get her psychiatric help, she seemed her old self again. It was as if the two week pall had just lifted.

"I'm going to have twins," Molly told him at supper. He stopped eating, holding his fork in mid-air and looked at her. "It's true," she said. "I have prayed and prayed for two weeks, and last night God answered me. I dreamed I was in the emergency room with stomach pains. Suddenly, I was giving birth. I had two girls and they were beautiful. When I woke up, I knew God was telling me this would really happen. He answered my prayers. Jake, don't you see?"

Jake sat there stunned. He just nodded in mute silence. He was glad to have his wife back. However, he believed she would someday be disappointed again. He hoped and prayed he was wrong.

Then, two months later, she announced she was going to have another baby.

When she got pregnant this third time, her husband did everything to make it easier for her. His patience with her was endless, and even though she only thought of the baby, he loved her. He was lonely and felt pushed aside, but said nothing.

Things will be normal again when the baby comes, he thought to himself.

Now *this* had to happen. Holding Molly's limp hand he knew this would end their marriage and emotionally kill his beloved wife.

"I love you, Molly," he said, as the tears rolled down his cheeks.

Chapter Three

Molly spent three more days in the hospital and insisted that Maggie, as she would be called, remain in the room with her. This was not standard procedure. However, Doctor Hook allowed it. He felt so bad for Molly and Jake that he thought this small infraction of the rules would help Molly a great deal. He was seeing signs of major depression and had suggested counseling for both of them. Molly would have no part of it.

"It could help you and Jake take better care of Maggie," Dr. Hook coaxed. "You want to do all you can for her, don't you?"

Even this tactic of doing it for her daughter didn't convince Molly. "I am not crazy," she cried. "If you had lost your baby, you'd be upset also."

Jake visited his wife daily, but he stayed for a shorter time with each visit. Molly would just stare out the window or begin to cry. She'd say very little; everything he tried to tell her would only remind her of her loss. When he picked Maggie up, or even cooed at her, Molly would become hysterical.

"Be careful; don't hurt her-she's all I've got left. "Don't do that-you'll scare her. Leave her alone-I don't want anything to happen to her."

Even when he left the baby alone, Molly would react.

"Go look at her. Is she still breathing? Why is she so quiet?"

Nothing he said or did made a difference to Molly. He tried everything to reach her, but she had built a wall around herself and he could not penetrate it.

When little Maggie was exactly three days old, she and her mother came home. Jake had scurried around during their stay in the hospital, cleaning and trying to make things as pleasant and as normal as possible. To his disappointment, Molly made no mention of the huge banner across the front of the house.

"WELCOME HOME MOLLY AND MAGGIE. I LOVE YOU BOTH" went unnoticed and unacknowledged. Molly carried Maggie through the sparkling house and up the stairs to her room, as if in a trance. Molly said nothing; her face remained blank and her eyes empty. Even the white roses, her favorite, beside her bed seemed invisible to her. Jake tried not to show his hurt as Molly placed their daughter in the bassinet beside her bed, moved the roses to the dresser, and got into bed herself.

"It's good to have you home," he kissed his wife. "I'll come check on you later. You rest now."

"It'll never be the same again," she began to sob. "Patricia should be here too. I don't think I can live without her."

"You'll feel better soon," he said. He hoped this would be true, but he was terribly worried about Molly's depression. "You rest now and I'll be back in a few hours." He gently closed the door and let the tears fall.

His mother had reassured him that all women go through a let-down after having a baby. She termed it "postpartum depression." "Molly will probably feel better in a month or two," his mother assured.

However, it had been almost four months now, and Molly seemed to be worse instead of better. She would not let Maggie out of her sight and panicked if the baby coughed. She still spoke of Patricia, sometimes ignoring Maggie's cries. Jake tried to help his wife, but he never knew how to take her.

"One minute she tells me to get that crybaby out of her sight, and the next moment she's screaming at me not to touch her," he whispered to the doctor. He had called Dr. Hook on the sly, knowing he would be seeing Maggie the next day. "Please, tell me what I can do?"

"Let me try to talk with her when I see her. Maybe I can convince her to get help," he responded.

It was time for Maggie's four month check-up and Molly actually looked close to her old self when Jake dropped them off. He was smiling as he went to park the car, which took him longer than usual.

Doctor Hook's office was in a building shared by three other doctors and two lawyers. The parking area was often packed with cars. He had learned that from one to three seemed less crowded, so made Maggie's appointment for one forty-five. However, today was unusually busy, and he ended up having to parallel park on one of the side streets.

He walked with a light feeling and a bounce in his step which he hadn't had in quite a while. Molly had smiled and thanked him when he brought her breakfast that morning. Later, she had come down stairs looking radiant in her blue and rose print dress that he had recently bought her. She had put on some makeup and lipstick. Maggie was gurgling in her arms, wearing her frilly pink dress with a hair bow to match.

Jake smiled. "Here come my two beautiful girls. It's good to see you looking so well, Mol." He spoke with an enthusiasm he thought he had lost.

There was still a remoteness and emptiness in her eyes he thought as he pulled up to the doctor's building, but she is getting better. Five minutes later he pushed his way out of the packed elevator at the fourth floor and entered Dr. Hook's waiting room.

Not seeing Molly, he checked in at the receptionist's desk and was told to go on back.

"Room two," she called to him, and acknowledging her with a wave, he strode down the hall.

He opened the door to find Molly alone, and in tears, and his heart sank.

"Where is the baby? Is she okay?" he cried. He couldn't imagine anything else that could get her so upset.

25

Before she could answer, the nurse entered with Maggie, noting as she did, that the baby was up to fourteen pounds and healthy in every way.

"The doctor will be back in a minute and then you will be free to leave," she spoke quietly .

Finally, after getting nothing out of his wife, Jake sat there blankly and waited for the doctor. After what seemed like an eternity, he entered with a prescription and a few samples which he held out to Molly. Getting no response, he handed the items to Jake and quietly repeated what he had told Molly.

"Physically, Molly is fine. She needs to get up and about. I am giving her some vitamins and a prescription for an antidepressant. You need to move Maggie to her own room now and share in her care. Molly must get on with her life. I also suggested a competent psychologist whom I think will help. Jake, let me give you her name in case Molly changes her mind about seeing her. She has had great success with postpartum parents. I am not saying Molly is crazy - just in need of some help. Please, Molly, won't you try to - She turned her back to him. He stopped and shrugged at Jake.

"Dr. Hook doesn't know what he is talking about," she screamed all the way home in the car. "He said I'm fine and need to get up and do things. I am not fine. Look at me; I just lost one baby and have another one who keeps me awake with her crying. I am tired and weak still. I simply need more time. He's a quack. I must find another physician!"

She ranted and raved all the way home about her doctor's advice and when Jake tried to tell her that maybe he was right, she accused him of being uncaring.

"How can you say that man could be right? Whose side are you on, anyway? I thought that at least you would care about me."

Not once in her long tirade did she mention his needs or, more importantly, the baby's.

When did she become so self-centered?, he wondered. He felt so helpless and alone.

That very day he moved Maggie to her nursery, ignoring Molly's pleas and tears. He knew the doctor was right, and he did want to spend more time with his daughter. In Molly's room he could not even get near the baby without her scrutiny. Jake had long since moved into the guest room.

"Please, God, let this help," he prayed as he placed his child in her own room and turned on the mobile hanging above the crib. It took Molly a week before she would speak to him again and even then it was only when it was necessary.

Wednesday of that week Molly suddenly informed him that she had found a new doctor, and he even made house calls.

"I saw his advertisement on television and called the 900 number he gave. He was very nice on the phone and assured me he could help me," she smiled.

He just stared in stunned silence unable to grasp what she was saying. Stuttering, he questioned, "Y-y-y-ou did what?"

"Found a new doctor. His name is Charles Simmons and he's very nice. He said he understood how I felt and could help me, so I called Dr. Hook's office and fired him. Jake, don't look at me like that. He makes house calls and will care for Maggie as well as me. Don't be such a worrier, for Christ's sake. It's for Maggie I'm switching."

All he could say was, "Fine!" and leave the room. *Like hell it's for Maggie*, he thought. *God, when is all this going to end?* He didn't know whom he was most angry at; her, himself, or God.

Dr. Charles Simmons arrived the following day. He was a tall man with graying brown hair and a well kept handle-bar mustache. His horn-rimmed glasses could not hide his beady brown eyes, and Jake instantly sized him up as a fraud. From then on "Dr. Charles" became her regular physician and friend. He claimed he was helping her and Molly adored him. Jake hated him and steered clear whenever he came around.

Jake had taken some time to inquire into the good doctor's background and, from what he found, combined with his gut instincts, Jake was convinced he was a quack. Simmons was telling his desperate wife what she wanted to hear, and prescribing pills that she "insisted" she needed, at her expense, of course. Whatever the "wonderful" doctor was doing for her was obviously not helping. Molly just seemed to get worse. Yet when Jake tried to express his concerns about "Dr. Charles", she would only snap at him and cry.

"Dr. Charles is the only one who cares enough to help me. He believes I'm sick, even if you don't. Whose side are you on, for Christ's sake?"

He threw up his hands and left the room, never mentioning his wife's illness again. However, he couldn't stop being concerned. Jake knew that deep down he still loved her very much. How he longed for the old Molly and the happy times they once had.

As the year went on, Molly began having migraines and feeling "sick" more and more often. She started accumulating pills, and taking them when she felt she needed them, not when she was supposed to, and not the prescribed dosage. She was staying in bed more and more frequently, and many days Jake would come home to find Maggie screaming for lack of attention. He now did most of the cooking and cleaning, and the stress was dragging him down. One day, he brought Molly her supper in time to see her take four of her migraine pills instead of the allotted two. He tried once more to tell her it could be quite dangerous not to follow the directions, but she just brushed him off.

"Mind your own business. I know what I'm doing. Besides, what do you care?"

At that point, all his frustration and rage surfaced, and he erupted like a volcano.

"Fine, if you want to kill yourself go ahead. But I don't have to watch," he yelled and stormed out of the room in a rage.

"I just can't take this anymore," he groaned. "What am I going to do?"

Leaning against the wall, tears filled his eyes. He felt like his whole world was slowly falling apart and he was helpless to stop it.

After standing in the hall for what seemed an eternity, Jake went into the nursery and looked down at his sleeping daughter. Maybe his wife was gone from him, but he still had Maggie. He just stood and stared down at his beautiful little girl. She was almost a year old now and so pretty. Her hair was becoming a mass of dark brown curls to match her brown eyes. She looked so peaceful lying on her stomach with her thumb in her mouth, holding on tight to the panda bear he had brought her last Christmas. He remembered the night in April when the bear had fallen behind her bureau and she couldn't find "Pandy". He had to search every corner of the room until he found the lost toy before she'd stop sobbing and gone to sleep. The two were inseparable. He smiled down at her and when she moved, he thought again of Molly and his loneliness. Suddenly, he realized what he was thinking and he shuddered. Feeling shocked and ashamed, Jake quickly left the nursery.

What am I thinking? She is only a baby. How can I feel this way?

Little did he know these fantasies would haunt him over the next few years, and eventually win out.

Chapter Four

Four Years Later

"Hi, princess, I'm home. Have you been in front of that thing all day? Where's Mom?"

Jake's sudden appearance startled his daughter. Maggie had been engrossed in one of her videos and didn't hear him come in. She got up to give him a quick, tentative hug, then returned to watching Snow White.

"Mommy's lying down," she responded. "She's having one of her sick headaches. I'm trying to be quiet like she told me. Sophie is still here and is making supper."

Jake just rolled his eyes. He understood what Maggie was saying. She had been alone most of the day. Molly was probably lying in bed, had the curtains shut, and did not want to see anybody. Over the past four years she had pulled more and more away from reality. One day, when Maggie was barely two years old, her loving mother had even tried to commit suicide.

"I'm sorry to interrupt, sir." His secretary, Juliann, was standing at the door to his office. "Your wife just called."

"What now?" he moaned. He had to finish the project he was working on. The deadline was five that afternoon and it was now almost noon. He had left strict orders not to be disturbed. However he could tell by Juliann's face this was serious enough for her to neglect his orders.

He liked and respected Juliann. She was a short, slender woman whom he guessed to be about forty-five. She would never tell her age and so had everyone in the office guessing. She had auburn hair containing a few gray threads, which was cut short and very becoming. Her bright blue eyes were always smiling and never missed anything.

She had come to him quite by accident three months ago when his former secretary decided to go back to school. He had called the secretarial pool. They informed him that they would be sending a young woman named Jolene. Evidently, someone got mixed up and they sent the wrong person. By the time they realized their mistake, he had fallen in love with Juliann and decided that their mistake was his good fortune. She had proven to be invaluable to him. Actually, he had to admit, she was the one who ran the office.

Now seeing the look on her face, Jake knew something was awry.

"Juli, what is it?" he could not hide the panic in his voice. "Is the baby all right? How's Molly?"

"It's Molly. She insists if you don't come home now she's going to kill herself. I tried to tell her you were very busy, but she wouldn't listen. I'm sorry to bother you, but I didn't know what to do. She really sounded desperate."

She knew all about the problems he and Molly were having, and felt so bad for her boss. There were many days she covered for him when he had to leave early. He seemed to have aged rapidly since she came here to work and she wished she could do more to help. He was only thirty years old, but lately he looked so much older. It was almost as if he was aging right before her eyes. She hated to see him like this. Many times he would come to work so down and depressed, that a pencil would break and he would cry out of pure frustration. Her heart would just break.

"I guess I had better go to her," he sighed as he put on his jacket. "It's probably nothing -she's *always* threatening to kill herself. It's just a way to get attention. Would you please type up the work

32

I have completed to this point? I'll be back as soon as I can." He left the office without looking back.

Picking up the strewn papers from his desk, Juliann quietly sobbed. *Mr. Stelson doesn't deserve this*, she thought, *I hope he will be all right.* This was the first time he showed absolutely no emotion and it scared her.

"What's going on?" Jake yelled, as he ran into his house. He drove up to see an ambulance out front and his front door opened wide. His voice was mixed with panic and rage.

"You the husband?"

Jake nodded.

Your wife has tried to kill herself," the paramedic said. He wasn't very sympathetic as far as Jake was concerned. He spoke as he and his partner pushed by Jake with the stretcher. "Apparently she called 911, stating she had taken an overdose. We rushed over and found her unconscious and her breathing shallow. She's still alive. Do you want to ride with us to the hospital?"

"What about my daughter?" Jake screamed, "Where is she?"

"We didn't know there was a child. We didn't see anyone else."

Jake took the stairs two at a time, and ran to Maggie's room where he found her quietly sleeping. He couldn't imagine how she could sleep through all the turmoil, but he was relieved. When he reached down to pick her up she was cold, clammy, and breathing very hard. Scared, he grabbed her and ran downstairs.

Paula, the second paramedic, spotted him and immediately reacted. Checking out the baby, she placed her on the stretcher with her mother.

"She doesn't seem as sick as her mom," Paula spoke softly and gently. "It may be that your wife simply gave her something to make her sleep. I don't think she was trying to kill her."

Jake rode beside Paula in a daze. He said nothing and just stared through blank eyes. He had a strong desire to just reach down and finish the job Molly had started. What was he going to do?

An hour or so later, Molly had been stabilized after having her stomach pumped and was resting comfortably. Maggie was asleep in the nursery.

"Your daughter is okay. She was given a mild sleeping pill," explained the doctor, a young Indian resident who looked like he had been sleeping in his clothes."We'd like to keep her overnight just to observe her and be sure she has no further reactions. Your wife is going to live, but we'd like to keep her here a few days. With your permission we'd like to bring a psychiatrist to work with her."

You have my permission," Jake responded halfheartedly. "I don't think it will do much good. I've suggested it before."

"I understand," said Dr. Hajra. "Let's give it a try anyway."

"Can I see my daughter?" Jake asked. He could not bear to go see Molly.

"She's asleep in the nursery, third floor. Try not to be too long."

After staying with his child for a few minutes, Jake rode the elevator down to the lobby and headed out. He was in a state of shock and walked like a zombie. Just two weeks earlier, they celebrated Maggie's second birthday. Molly actually joined in the frivolity and Jake's hope began to increase. *Maybe this is a good sign,* he contemplated. *Maybe she's getting better.* How wrong he had been!

He arrived at the office about four o'clock looking like he had been hit by a truck, and not even realizing how he had gotten there. Juliann just watched in silence as he walked past her into his domain. A few minutes later, she entered with a cup of fresh coffee to find him sitting with his head in his hands.

"Juli, what am I going to do?" he asked without even looking up. "I can't go on like this."

Work was becoming quite hectic lately and he was really tense. People simply weren't buying computers as often as they used to. Since the later models were better built and longer lasting, folks were more interested in finding new and creative software and computer programs which, at this time, Stelson and Co. weren't able to provide. His dad had been approached with an offer from a

well known competitor to buy Stelson and Co. and he was seriously considering selling.

Jim Stelson II opened his company when computers were a new
concept and business skyrocketed. He was able to double his
father's inheritance in just two years. Five years after opening the
company he was a millionaire and then some. Jake joined his dad
after college, and since then his job had been to come up with new
and innovative ideas to help them stay ahead of the competition. It
had proven to be hard work lately, especially with a sick wife and
small child he hadn't had the same drive to go the extra mile. Again
today, his dad 'suggested' he take some time off to get his act
together. His feeling of helplessness, which was slowly becoming
the normal feeling, had returned.

"I have to get this project done. My wife and daughter are in the
hospital. Maggie will be coming home tomorrow without her mother. I can't afford to miss any more work. Dad is already on my back
about my work slipping. I feel like just giving up on everything."

His shoulders were shaking and Juliann realized all too well
the anguish he felt. All she seemed able to do was keep her hand
on his shoulder. Words escaped her and her heart ached for him.

Juliann Mary Quarles had been a widow for seven years. She
would never forget her husband's death as long as she lived. It was
the evening of their twentieth wedding anniversary celebration . It
was late, actually early morning, and they had just arrived home
after a lovely evening of partying.

Filled with a totally wonderful feeling of joy, Juli was relaxing
in a warm tub. All their friends and family had been there. Her
daughter Sandy, and sons Paul and Steve, had pulled it all together on the sly, with the help of Juliann's sister. They had told her
and Adam that they wanted to take them out for a quiet dinner at
their favorite restaurant, Richards. Upon arriving, they were
escorted to a back room. She nearly lost her teeth when the doors
opened and they were bombarded with shouts of joy, handshakes,
and hugs. It was a wonderful surprise and Adam had talked about
it all the way home. "They shouldn't have done it," he kept saying.

"It was too much; they shouldn't have." Thinking back, she realized there was more to his words than simple concern for his children.

She had just finished thinking, "What did I do to be so blessed?" when she heard it. It was as if a bomb had exploded outside her door. The noise was deafening. She jumped up, grabbed her robe, and ran down the stairs dripping wet where she saw him. Her quiet, unassuming, gentle "soul mate" had shot himself through the right temple.

She survived for five years with the help of booze, then one day she awoke in the detox center of the hospital and saw the fear in her daughter's eyes. Then and there, she vowed to change. She entered a drug rehabilitation program, joined AA, and went back to school. The oldest in her business class, she was teased but accepted, and graduated second in her class. Sandy was the one who suggested she get into a temporary agency so that she could get different types of jobs, and thus experience. She did, and it wasn't long before she was sent to work for Mr. Stelson. He was wonderful to work for, and the two of them seemed to click from the first day. She loved working for him and knew how much he admired her work. They quickly became a team. She remembered well her second day when he stuck his head out of his office door and said, "Guess what? I just got a call from the secretary pool. They said they had accidentally sent up the wrong person. Would I like to make a change?" Jolene, their original choice had much more experience."

With her heart in her mouth, she tried to read his face. It was true her experience was minimal, but she thought she had been doing okay. Would he send her back?

Then he grinned and said, "I told them 'no thanks -you sent me the best.'" He ducked back into his office and she slumped in her chair with a sigh of sheer pleasure.

That was only three months ago, but she felt like she had been here forever. Now,all she could do was stand and feel for him and understand.

The silence was broken suddenly when the phone started ringing. Both of them were brought back to reality with a start and Juli reached to pick it up.

"Hello", she spoke tentatively.

"Juliann, this is Emily Stelson. I just heard the news. Is my son available?" She had such a quiet, dignified voice.

"Just a minute, please," Juli responded formally. With her hand on the receiver she spoke quietly to her boss. "It's your mother. She knows what happened and wants to talk with you."

He wasn't surprised. His mother always seemed to know things before he could tell her. He took the phone from her, and Juliann gently closed the door behind her as she left.

Juli looked up tentatively when she heard his door open. On his face was a look of relief and she relaxed. She knew his mother could be quite demanding and overpowering.

"A friend of hers in the emergency room called her," he spoke quietly. "She offered to help by taking Maggie for a few days and gave me the numbers of a few reputable agencies where I may be able to find a live-in housekeeper. She strongly suggested I call."

Juliann saw a bit of hope in her boss' eyes and smiled.

"I called Dad", he continued, "and got a three day extension on the Tyler project. I'm going to take tomorrow off and interview people. I'd like to find someone before Molly comes home."

The next day Jake started calling the agencies his mom had told him about, and two days later Sophie joined their family.

Along with four other places, his mother had suggested Temps, Inc. This agency was the first to return Jake's call to say they had someone they felt would fit his needs. He was relieved and made an appointment for that afternoon.

At precisely one o'clock the doorbell rang. There stood a striking, middle-aged, Spanish woman. Her hair was jet black with a few gray strands woven through it. She had large brown eyes and olive skin. She was stocky and had a very kind face. She held out her hand and introduced herself as Sophie. He invited her to come in and sit down and after the first ten minutes knew he liked her.

Sophie was pleasant and self-assured. She had good references and a quiet, gentle manner about her. Somehow Jake knew he could trust her and decided to be completely honest with her. He explained his wife's illness and that he believed it was all psychological. He emphasized how Molly could be very demanding and critical one day, but sulky and whiny the next.

"She'll be in the hospital a few more days. She can be extremely demanding and it can get very stressful. You never know what you'll find upon entering her room," he told her. " Also, her voice can sound sweet and pleasant, but her words are condescending and biting. I feel you should know, because there will be times when you may feel that she is your friend and other days she'll blame you and curse you. She is very possessive of Maggie and becomes upset if anyone tries to help, yet often neglects her completely. I just don't know what to do anymore," he moaned, as if talking to himself, not Sophie.

The pain and heartache of the past few months were obvious to Sophie, and she feared for him. Her experiences told her this would probably get worse before it got better.

She waited until he regained control. She knew that the last thing he needed was to be embarrassed by his sudden show of weakness. When he was ready, she assured him she could do the job and Molly's difficult behavior didn't frighten her. She had worked in difficult situations before.

"I can be pretty thick-skinned," she told him. " I grew up with an alcoholic father and his moods could change at the drop of a hat. I have to tell you, though, I will be tough and tell her exactly what I think. I am not afraid of confrontation."

Jake Stelson was impressed with this woman and hired her immediately. He wondered if she would be the one to finally reach Molly.

Sophie Martinez started that very day by cooking supper for him and picking up the house. She had told him she preferred to commute, but would be happy to stay any night he truly needed her to. Her apartment was not far and she could get there quickly if he called.

When Jake brought Maggie home the following day, she took to Sophie immediately. The housekeeper fell head over heels in love with the beautiful child. Even Molly seemed to respond to her. That was four years ago, and she had proven to be all that he had hoped for and more.

Jake stopped at the kitchen to inform Sophie he was home, then headed upstairs to shower and change into something comfortable.

It was extremely relaxing just standing under that hot shower and letting his tired shoulders be massaged with the pounding water. Jake wanted to stay there forever. It was only his sense of responsibility that finally convinced him to get out.

After getting into comfortable clothes, he dared to go see Molly. The room was dark, as he expected, and smelled stale and old.

"Molly, are you awake?" he went over to her bed. "I just got home and Maggie said you weren't feeling well. Anything I can get for you?"

"Yeah, get out," she moaned. "It's your fault. You killed my babies. You don't really care. So just leave me alone."

The slur in her voice told Jake she had taken too much medication. She had pills for everything; depression, migraines, insomnia. He had teased her once that she could open her own pharmacy, but she accused him of being unsympathetic and didn't speak to him for a week.

He knew it was fruitless, but he had to try again.

"Sweetheart, you have a daughter. She and I both love you and need you. Please come join us for supper."

"You don't care a bit about me - now get out!" she yelled as she hurled a pillow at him. "I don't want to eat - I want to die. Wouldn't you be sorry if you came in and found me dead ? It would serve you right. Maybe tonight I'll do it."

"You don't want to do that," he pleaded. Promise me you won't. See - I'm going. Please, Molly, I won't bother you again - I promise."

"Okay , you win, but I sure feel like ending it. Now leave!"

He softly closed the door behind him, and sadly went to join his daughter in the living room. He hated going into his wife's room any more. He knew she'd never kill herself, but would come close. She had tried one other time since Sophie came, but luckily the housekeeper was there and able to stop her before she took all her pills. Sometimes he thought she used those dreaded words just to manipulate him. He hated himself for letting her, but didn't seem to have the energy to fight her.

Why is all this happening to me? he wondered. *What did I ever do to deserve all this pain?*

Returning to the living room, he quietly walked to his favorite easy chair and fell into it. Sitting there feeling lonely and empty, he watched his little daughter as she lay on the floor absorbed in her movie.

She was growing up so fast and becoming quite pretty. She seemed to him to be already better looking than Molly. She had her mother's deep brown eyes and hair. She had his strong chin and dimples and would eventually have his height. She was going to be beautiful some day, but then again, maybe he was just prejudiced. After all, he loved her very, very much. She reminded him so much of her mother when he first met her, before she got "sick".

"Come on, princess. Sit on daddy's lap," he coaxed.

"I can see better from here," she whined.

Maggie didn't want to do that. She wasn't exactly sure why, but she no longer liked sitting with her daddy. Until about a year ago, she loved to curl up in his lap, he would hug her tight and tell her stories to make her laugh, and she felt so safe. Then something changed. He started doing things she didn't like. Now, at age five, Maggie could not tell anyone, but she no longer loved being alone with her daddy.

"Oh, come on, sweetie. We'll snuggle up under the blanket and watch the movie together."

Reluctantly, she crawled up onto his lap as Jake wrapped the blanket around her.

"Now isn't this better than the floor?" he whispered in her ear.

For a few minutes it was like before, Maggie hoped this time would be different. It began again. His hand reached down and he began to touch and fondle her genitals. Even at her young age, she felt it was wrong and uncomfortable. But this was her daddy, and he wouldn't do anything to hurt her, would he? She felt very confused and wanted to run and hide.

"Now doesn't this feel good?" he asked, as he stroked her bottom. "Come on, you know you like it. It's your fault, you know. You are just so pretty and I love you so much. I know you won't tell anybody our secret, will you? Besides, no one will believe you. They'll tell you you're a bad girl and God will punish you." She barely heard him, but managed to say yes.

Maggie cringed as he continued to caress her and she wished she could just disappear. She began to fantasize that she was Snow White and her prince came and swooped her up and carried her off. This always helped and it didn't hurt so much. She could forget.

"Well, don't you two look cozy?"

The words brought her back to reality and she saw Sophie standing there smiling at them. She wanted so much to run into Sophie's arms and tell her what he was doing under the blanket. She started to get up and he held her close.

Why can't anybody see? she thought. *If it's okay, how come it has to be a secret?*

Deep down, Maggie believed Jake's words and knew it was her fault and she was bad. She did not want God or her father to punish her, so she would not tell anyone. She was afraid because sometimes it did feel good to her and that scared her. More and more, her fantasies became realities, and the "real" Maggie hid deeper and deeper inside her. From now on, she would be good and quiet and try to disappear.

"Well, supper is about ready," Sophie spoke again. "Why don't you two get ready and I'll bring Molly her tray?"

Jake released Maggie with a pat on the bottom and lightly told her to go wash up. He hated himself when he did that to her, but for some reason, he just couldn't stop himself. He knew it bothered her, he felt her tense up in his arms, so he had to convince her it

41

would be wrong to tell anyone. He dreaded what would happen if anyone found out the truth. Someday, when she was old enough, he would tell her he was sorry and explain his need for her and for her love. She was a bright girl and she would understand. Little did he realize how he was pushing her further and further away.

After he left the nursery that night four years ago, he often had thoughts of using Maggie to fulfill his need for love and tenderness. He would reprimand himself at these disgusting thoughts, but the feelings constantly got stronger. He tried staying away from her and only holding her when someone else was in the room.

Then, when she was four, he couldn't control himself any longer. It was the evening of her fourth birthday, and he was tucking her in bed. Sophie had just given her a bath, and when he bent to kiss her good night he could smell the powder and shampoo scents and something snapped. He lay beside her and put his arm around her and started telling her a story.

"Once there was a beautiful princess called Maggie and her daddy loved her very much..."

Maggie loved her daddy and smiled up at him as he spoke. He could tell the most wonderful stories.

Then he did something she didn't understand. He pulled up her nightie and began to touch her. She was scared, but knew it was her daddy, so said nothing.

"And the princess let the prince love her in a special, secret way and promised never to tell his secret to anyone." He went on as he kissed her bottom, " The prince and princess lived happily ever after."

Maggie cried herself to sleep that night, but didn't know why. She was confused and afraid. "Is this the way a daddy is supposed to love his little girl?" After that, Jake would go to her room frequently.

Maggie ran into the bathroom and locked the door. Tears flowed as she washed not only her hands, but all of her. She wanted so badly to stay there forever and never come out. She was so confused and felt so lonely. She was only five and had no one to love her as she needed. She couldn't tell anyone. She sat down beside the closed door and listened. She would at least wait for Sophie to go back downstairs, then she wouldn't have to be alone with him.

"Supper, Molly. Are you awake?"

She heard Sophie's quiet knock and gentle voice at her mother's door. How she wished Sophie could be her mother. Her mommy was sick all the time. When Maggie asked her to go to the park or someplace, her answer was always the same.

"Not today, sweetie - mommy has a bad headache. Why don't you go watch TV?"

Maggie couldn't even remember a time when her mommy wasn't sick in bed. She was always so sad, and told Maggie the best thing she could do for her was try to be very quiet.

Lots of times Maggie could hear her mommy and daddy screaming at each other.

"You have been this way ever since Maggie was born. When is it going to end? Enough is enough!" her daddy yelled one day.

"You bastard!" Mommy screamed. "You know how much her birth upset me. Why can't you understand my feelings?"

The argument went on and on, and got louder and louder. Maggie began to believe that it was all her fault that Mommy was sick and Daddy was sad. From then on, she tried to be really good and keep really quiet. She had to show them she was not really bad. However, deep inside of her, she knew she was.

"I'm not hungry," her mother's voice growled. "Leave me alone."

"Molly, you need to eat and get your strength."

Sophie's words were gentle but stern, as she entered the stale dark room. Setting down the tray, she went over to open the shades and let in the final sunlight of the day.

"Boy, it's dreary in here. No wonder you feel depressed. This darkness and gloom could depress anyone. Now, sit up and eat before it gets cold. I'll come back for your tray and I expect to find nothing left."

When the housekeeper left, Molly began to eat as if she hadn't tasted food in days. She didn't stop until the last crumb was gone. She never would have admitted how hungry she was to anyone, and she would never let anyone see her sneak down for something to eat, which she often did when the house was dark and everyone was asleep.

Molly would never admit this either, but she liked and admired Sophie. She was strong and kind, yet took no nonsense. She was the only one that would stand up to Molly and tell her what to do, and secretly, Molly liked her for this. Jake was such a wimp and would always give in to her whining. He was just so weak. Every time he tried to coax her to get up, she wanted to throw something at him. She would deny it if someone said it to her but she longed for him to yell at her and tell her off. She thought that, maybe if he were strong, she would be also. All he did, however, was give in and leave her. How she longed for him to hold her close and tell her he loved her! She needed him, but would never tell him outright. If he couldn't figure that out then he didn't deserve her love.

Molly thought of her daughter. Maggie, her little Mags, was her pride and joy. Surely, Maggie knew that. When she sent for Maggie, she came in smiling and crawled under the blankets beside her. Molly would tell her how she loved her and how special she was. She would tell Maggie she loved her more than anyone else, even Daddy. It was Daddy's fault that Maggie had no sisters and brothers. Because he didn't care, two babies died before her. Molly would tell her young daughter about Patty, her twin sister who died so she could live.

"How special and beautiful Patty was!" she would mutter. Maggie would lay near her mommy, quiet and still believing it was her fault Patty died. No wonder no one loved her. How could she be so bad? She was only five.

Molly smiled as she pushed her tray aside.

Yes, she thought, *my little girl loves me, I'm sure of that. She will never betray me, as her father did.*

Maggie heard Sophie come out of the room and start downstairs. She quietly closed the door behind her and tiptoed into the kitchen. She wished she could be invisible.

Sophie sat and ate with them, as she often did, and the three of them talked and laughed as if all was wonderful. Actually, Sophie and Jake talked about adult gossip and how the world was falling apart. Maggie, sat and stared at her plate, playing with her mashed potatoes. No one seemed to notice her and she was glad. No one noticed this little girl withdrawing from their world.

They don't even care, she cried inside. *They don't even care.*

Chapter Five

Three weeks later Maggie was up bright and early. This was her first day of kindergarten; she was excited and frightened at the same time. Sophie had taken her to the store the week before and bought her a brand new "Snow White" lunch box, new shoes, and a pretty new school dress.

"Mommy, look what I got for my school!" She bounded into her mother's room full of excitement.

"Not now, Maggie - I have a terrible headache. I'll look later, I promise."

Maggie refused to let the tears that welled in her eyes fall as she quietly closed the door and walked to her own room. She let her new things drop on the bed, no longer caring about them.

"God, please make mommy well, and let her like me," she whispered. After a while, she walked downstairs to watch TV.

"Did your mom like your new things?" asked Sophie. Molly had asked Sophie to take the child downtown.

"I just can't do it. Please, my head hurts so bad I can hardly lift it. Please, do it for me, Sophie," Molly had whined when Sophie protested that it wasn't her job to take Maggie school shopping. In the end, Sophie agreed to do it, not for Molly, but for Maggie.

"Yeah, she said they were great," Maggie lied. Even at the tender age of five, Maggie had learned how to cover up her pain. She quickly understood that it was better to say what she thought people wanted to hear rather than what she truly felt. It made people happy, and she desperately wanted everyone in the house to be happy.

She laid in bed that night telling herself she would do all the right things in school, and everyone would be proud of her, and love her. If she was real good, maybe Mommy and Daddy would stop fighting all the time, and Mommy would get better.

Suddenly, her door opened. She knew without looking up, what it meant.

"You all ready for tomorrow?" he cooed as he came nearer. "Let me tuck you in, and you can tell me all about the new things you bought."

He left an hour later, and all she could do was roll over and cry herself to sleep.

"Please, Daddy, please, I'll be good. Please stop." She drifted off to sleep.

When she awoke, Daddy had already left for work, and Sophie was there to take her to school.

The first day of kindergarten was difficult for Maggie. She was scared and lonely. Her daddy had to finish up a brand new project he had been working on. Juli would be waiting for him and he couldn't change their plans now. He never could. Of course, her mom was too sick to go with her.

Sophie held her hand as she stood in the doorway of the brightly decorated class.

"You'll have fun, baby," the housekeeper said to her. Maggie just looked up with tears in her eyes and shrugged.

"Hi, you must be Maggie. She'll be fine, Mrs. Stelson. We'll take good care of this pretty little girl. You can pick her up at noon."

The teacher walked away before Sophie could correct her, and Maggie walked away in silence with her new teacher.

Miss Trent was a kind, gentle, woman and a superb kindergarten teacher. All the kids liked her. She was about five' one", and full of energy. Her hair was naturally curly, shoulder-length, and bright coppery red. She had freckles galore, and would often let the kids try to guess how many she had. Her green eyes sparkled beneath her wire-rimmed glasses, and she was always smiling.

As far as Maggie was concerned, there was nothing Miss Trent could not do Maggie loved the free hugs and constant praise. Each morning the class would sing songs, and paint pictures, and learn letters and numbers. She always had some special paper or project to bring home.

Everyday at noon Sophie would be waiting for her at the bus stop to walk her home. All the kids were convinced she was Maggie's mother, and Maggie never bothered to correct them.

"What nice things did you do today?" Sophie asked as Maggie ate the sandwich which was always waiting for her.

"Nothing much," she'd answer with her mouth full. Then Sophie would check her lunch box to see if she had eaten her snack, and always found papers stuffed in it. She'd "oooh" and "ah" over the pictures and always coaxed Maggie to show her mom.

"Maggie, you should show these to your mom. I know she'd love to see them. She seems better today, really."

"Okay, I might," was Maggie's constant response.

Finishing her lunch, she'd head upstairs. She'd stop in and say hi to her mom for a few minutes.

"I'm home, mommy." She'd walk over and give her mom a kiss.

"Hi, sweetie - how was school today? What did you do?"

"It was okay. We didn't do nothing much."

Always the same question, always the same answer. Maggie knew from her mom's voice that she didn't really care. She just asked. After all, mothers were *supposed* to ask.

Soon Molly would send her away. Maggie would go to her room and throw her papers into a cardboard box in her closet.

Maybe, someday they'll care, she thought.

Each day when Maggie left, Molly would kick herself.

"Why can't I get her to share more? I wait all morning for her to come home. I miss her so much. Then I try to be enthusiastic, but I don't know how anymore. Maybe she and Jake would be better off without me."

Jake never seemed to be around. He would leave for work early and get home late. He claimed he was working on different projects and had to meet deadlines. Yet last week when his mother stopped by to visit, she told Molly things were slow at work. Jake's father was seriously considering selling out to the competition. Molly was convinced she was pushing him away, and wished she could fix things. She didn't care about herself, but Maggie needed him. Little did she know that Maggie was much more relaxed when he wasn't there.

By October Maggie was telling her mom more and more about school and even showing her her papers. She was beginning to believe her Mommy did care. Molly kept telling her that she was feeling better and soon things would be a lot better.

At the end of the month, she beamed in her "Snow White" costume as she entered her mom's room.

"Sophie helped me make it. Do you think I look like a real princess?"

"You look beautiful." Her mother spoke with sincere admiration and Maggie knew she meant it. She threw her arms around her mother's neck and squeezed her tight. "I love you, Mommy," she whispered through her smile.

Tears rolled down her cheeks as Molly hugged her beautiful little girl.

"Oh Maggie, I will make things better for you,-I promise."

It was only three days later. Maggie hopped off the bus excitedly. "Sophie, next week we're having open house at school. We're going to sing two songs and say a poem for all the people who come. Do you think Mommy and Daddy will come? Maybe, Mommy will help me learn this poem. Do you think?"

Maggie stopped talking and looked up at Sophie. Her face was serious and her eyes were red. She just stared straight ahead and didn't say anything else. Maggie felt like throwing up and she didn't even know why. She just knew something had happened. When they got home there was no sandwich waiting for her and Sophie just sat her on her lap and began to stroke her hair.

"Sweetie, your mom is very sick in the hospital. She... " Maggie heard no more. Later, she woke up in her mom's bed and couldn't even remember how she got there.

It was dark when she walked downstairs, and her dad was in the kitchen talking with Grandmother Stelson. They stopped abruptly when she walked in and her grandmother gently carried her to her bed and tucked her in. Maggie couldn't even protest. She awoke in the morning with Sophie gently shaking her.

"No school today, darling. You're daddy just came home and said your mommy is going to be fine. You can go see her tomorrow."

Maggie closed her eyes again and went back to sleep with a smile on her face.

Chapter Six

It was Pat who found Molly that fateful day in early November, 1974. Four and a half years earlier, her former boss had had to let Molly go from the company. Her behavior had become sporadic and Pat could no longer depend on her. All the customers who patronized Patty's Pleasantries, a now-famous catering business, had started complaining about missed appointments, food not arriving, and so on.

She hated having to fire Molly, but had invested a great deal into the business and couldn't jeopardize it. She had promised Molly her job back when she got well again.

Patricia Walsch grew up in Brooklyn where her mom had run a small diner for years. Her dad had opened the diner a year before they were married and worked hard to keep it going. He was quite successful, it seemed. Then without warning, shortly after Pat turned seven, he took off, leaving her mom alone with three small children. Her mother worked long hard hours to keep the business going, and Pat became the caretaker at home. She never saw her father again.

The family was poor, since most of the money had to go back into the diner, so Pat learned to be creative when making meals. She enjoyed cooking and her sister and brother seemed to like what she made for them. Mom would often eat at the diner, which was right next to the apartment building where they lived. Sometimes she wouldn't get home until very late. Many nights, Pat would wait up for her, but the little ones would always be in bed when she arrived home, exhausted, and wondering if it was all worth it.

Claire M. Ford

"Why did your father do this to us?" she would moan and rub her aching feet. "If only I could get my hands on him now."

"Oh, Mama, we're better off without him," Patty would always answer her. "You'll feel better tomorrow."

Those nights Patty would let her mother vent her frustrations, then go to bed hating her father.

"You goddam son of a bitch," she'd yell into the darkness. "How could you be so cruel and selfish? I hate you more than you'll ever know." It would be way into the wee hours of the morning before she'd drift off into a fitful sleep.

Still she had to rise early to be there for her younger siblings. Somehow, though, they seemed to be more sensitive to her feelings and tried to be extra quiet. Through those years they came to depend on her more than the mother they hardly ever saw.

Even now, as adults, they tended to seek out Pat when they needed advice.

Pat struggled hard to finish high school, then started going to the diner to help her mom with the cooking and studying by correspondence at night. Eventually, she earned an associate degree in business management and dreamed of opening her own restaurant. She saved all she earned like a miser, and at age thirty had enough for a down payment on a small catering business on the corner two blocks away.

"It won't work," people warned her. "The location is bad and you'll lose your money. Why do you think the owner is selling?"

Patty bought it just the same. Her creativity and ingenuity soon changed people's minds. After two years, Patty needed a bigger place, and also felt she needed to be out on her own. Mom had been able to hire some help, and was seeing someone quite steadily now. Pat liked George, who was very good to her mother, and hoped someday the two would be married.

Mom deserves a break, Pat thought. *She's had a tough life.*

For a brief moment, the anger she felt for her dad surfaced again, but she quickly put him out of her mind.

Her siblings were grown, so now was Pat's chance. She knew she had to act. *But how?* she wondered. *Where?*

54

It was a visitor from western New York, who put her in touch with a gentleman in Buffalo, who was trying to rent spaces in a new mall he had designed.

An older woman entered Pat's shop and it seemed the woman could read Pat's thoughts. "Oooh, this is such a cute place," she cooed. "My niece, whom I'm visiting, raves about your pastries, and since I am blessed with twenty or so sweet teeth, I had to come in. You know, you look like you could use a bigger place. I know it would be quite a move, but up in Buffalo where I live, a brand new mall is about to open up. A close friend of mine designed it and is trying to rent space. I bet you'd be an instant success. Here's his card. Think about it. I just know you'd love it up there."

Pat read the business card: "Mr. Walter Williamson, designer and manager of Buffalo Mall. Phone number 555-3401." It didn't take Patty long to think about. It was as if opportunity had just dropped into her lap and she jumped at the chance. It was over twenty successful years ago that Pat had made the decision to move.

Pat had just completed her eighth year in Buffalo when Molly Harris walked into her shop looking for a job. She had no experience, but was willing to be trained, and seemed very sincere. She had only finished high school and was now nineteen, but loved math and economics best. Pat liked her right away and hired her. Molly had proven to be a good and faithful worker, and her endless energy and charisma were what seemed to draw the customers.

Pat had started Molly out as a receptionist. Her responsibilities included making appointments and answering the phone. However, Molly proved to be very conscientious and learned remarkably fast. Eventually, Pat promoted Molly to the position of catering representative. She was now in charge of talking to people, setting dates, and helping them to plan for the event they needed catered. She even had her own office. People would ask for her by name.

It was the year before Molly became ill that Pat had considered making her a partner. They had become fast friends and Pat knew

Molly would always be an asset to the company even though she was only twenty-six.

Pat had liked Molly very much and missed her terribly. She made it a point to visit Molly at least once a week, and would stay a few hours, helping with the baby, and trying to coax Molly into getting help.

Pat never saw Jake because Molly insisted she come in the mornings while he was at work. She never even knew if Molly had told Jake about her visits. She felt sorry for him also. She really liked him and his family, who often hired her company to cater their gala affairs. In fact, it was while they were catering one such affair, that Molly and Jake met.

Molly was working on some preliminary ideas to present to a perspective client wishing to cater a wedding, when she was summoned to her boss' office. Molly walked slowly down the hall, wondering why she was being called to the inner sanctum. Most times, Pat would just come to her.

"Sit down Molly." Her boss pointed to a nearby chair, and Molly sat tentatively, trying to read the woman's face.

Poised stiffly in the chair, Molly Harris hoped her shock over what was said to her didn't show too much.

"Molly, we just got a call to cater a family reunion for one of our steady clients, the Stelsons. I'd like to assign this project to you. What I'm saying is, that I want you to work this party yourself." Pat grinned at her young employee who had proven to be a definite asset to the business.

"I-I-I can't," stuttered Molly. "It's one of your most important clients. Oh, I don't want to lose them on you!"

"Nonsense, Molly. You've been learning fast and nothing gets past those pretty brown eyes of yours. I've told you that you'd make a great representative and planner - well, here's your chance. You have to start somewhere. I'm tied up with the Ilbento family banquet so I couldn't possibly do it. It's your baby now. I will not take no for an answer!" Pat walked away.

Molly walked into her little office, closed the door, and cried out of pure joy. "I can do a good job, Pat - you wait and see."

After standing for a minute she turned her attention to her assignment, and did, indeed, do a stupendous job.

"Excuse me," Molly turned toward the tall blond man who had walked up beside her and smiled. "Can I help you, sir?"

"I was told you were the person who 'threw' this grand affair together. I just wanted to say you did a magnificent job. I'd hire you in a minute. Can we have dinner together sometime?"

Molly smiled shyly. "That's the best pick-up I've had in a long time. However, as I say, 'flattery will get you everywhere', and I'd like to have lunch with you. My name is Molly Harris." She held out her hand, looking this handsome man squarely in the eye.

"I'm James Stelson, and my parents are your clients," he spoke as he took her hand. He was instantly in love with her wit and easy-going spirit. It didn't take him long to fall in love with the rest of her as well.

Molly turned ashen with the words. Why would someone so rich and famous be interested in her? What would they have in common? Suddenly, she wanted to take back what she had just said, but looking into his bright blue eyes, she couldn't get her mouth to work. He left her with the promise that he'd call soon.

True to his word, Jake, as his friends called him, telephoned her the following day and offered to take her to dinner. He picked her up from work at four thirty, drove her home so she could change, and took her to a fancy Italian restaurant on the north side of Buffalo. It was called Rolanio's, and it was wonderful.

They talked half the night, and it didn't seem to bother him that her father was a mechanic who ran his own garage/gas station, and her mom worked as a nursing assistant in a small nursing home in Rochester. In fact, Molly got the impression that he preferred to forget his wealth. He seemed to be uncomfortable being a scion of a prominent family and the heir to millions.

After that night, Jake and Molly became an item. His family liked her instantly. The fact she was "poor" and from the wrong side of the tracks didn't seem to faze them. The difference never even occurred to them.

"They were nothing like I expected, and they accepted me without question. I was sure they'd think I wasn't 'good enough' for their wealthy son, or think I loved only his money," She said excitedly to her mother one night. "Anyway, we'll be up to see you and Daddy on Saturday. You'll love Jake as much as I do - I know you will."

Sure enough, Molly's family simply adored Jake. In fact, at one rare moment when only the three of them were in the kitchen, her folks confided in her. "Young lady, if you don't marry that boy, we're planning to adopt him, so you'd better make up your mind fast." Her dad winked at her and sauntered back into the crowded living room. Her mom just smiled broadly and congratulated her. Giving her a great big bear hug, she whispered, "Oh Molly, he's everything we've ever wished for you. I am so happy you found such a good man." Molly could only chuckle to herself as she watched that dear woman who had given her birth twenty short years ago rejoin the festivities in the other room.

She laughed aloud, and that night told Jake their plans.

"I bet it'll be fun having two sets of parents," he grinned slyly. "I think I'll accept their offer."

"Don't even think about it," she jabbed him with her elbow. "You'd make a lousy brother."

"Yeah, you're right. However, I bet I'd make a terrific husband. Marry me?"

Molly just leapt into his arms and kissed him again and again.

"I take that as a 'yes'. He broke away from her to look into her laughing eyes.

A year later Pat catered their wedding reception as a wedding gift, ignoring Molly's constant protests. Molly looked absolutely radiant.

Since Maggie's birth, Pat watched her friend change from the bubbly, youthful, person she was- to a selfish, manipulative, very troubled woman. Pat knew it was the drugs and seclusion and tried to tell Molly this, but Molly wouldn't hear of it. Sometimes, Molly would force her to leave, or get really vulgar with her, but Pat continued to come back as she knew Molly wanted her to come. She was patient because she knew the real Molly and the woman she met on her weekly visits was not the Molly she knew.

Then, on one of her normal Tuesday visits, Pat found her young friend.

"It's me, Sophie", she called as she came in. Molly had given her a key long ago. "How is she today?"

Pat and Sophie had become confidants over the years since both wanted to help Molly. They often conspired on what to say, or do, sharing reactions and feelings. It seemed to Sophie that recently Molly was starting to listen.

"She seems a little better today," said Sophie, coming out of the kitchen to greet Pat. "I brought her breakfast around eight, and she was sitting up and had brushed her hair. She still talks about missing Maggie, but it didn't seem the same to me. I hope I'm not seeing what's not there."

It was a new blow for Molly when Maggie started school. It was as if she was losing her baby again and for the first few months she spoke to no one. Then, after a lot of coaxing from Sophie, Maggie started going to Molly's room and telling her stories about kindergarten, causing Molly to perk up a bit. Now she lived for one o'clock when Maggie would come to see her.

"Well, I'll go up and see if I can convince her to get dressed today," Pat smiled. She liked Sophie very much.

"Come in the kitchen for coffee before you leave. I have fresh baked cookies, also."

"I'll do that. I really should start selling your cookies in my shop. They're scrumptious."

"Molly - oh my God, Molly!" she yelled. Opening the door, she spotted Molly laying as if she were asleep, her hand hanging over the side of the bed holding an empty pill jar. "Sophie, help!" she yelled down the stairs, then reached for the phone.

She had just hung up after calling 911 when Sophie arrived at the door.

"She's overdosed," Pat cried. "An ambulance is on its way."

"I should have seen something. I should have noticed," Sophie cried as she helped Pat. They were still trying to revive her when the ambulance arrived and the paramedics immediately started CPR.

I hope it's not too late, Pat thought, as she watched her friend being placed on the stretcher.

Sophie went to call Jake at work, and Pat went with Molly in the ambulance.

When Molly came to she was in a private room at Buffalo Memorial Hospital, and Jake was gently holding her hand.

Her first thought was her baby and she sobbed, "Maggie - where's Maggie?"

"She's okay," Jake whispered. "She's at home with Sophie. In a few days when you are stronger I'll bring her to visit you. Do you remember anything?"

"I remember wanting to die, to make things easier for you and Maggie. I knew I was a burden on everyone, but couldn't think of a way out, except to kill myself. I remember swallowing a bunch of pills, then I woke up here. Where am I?"

"You're in the hospital and you'll be okay. Doctor Samson is the physician in charge of your case and he says you're very lucky. Molly, please let them help you."

She laid back and closed her eyes. Jake sat there for a while until a nurse asked him to leave so that his wife could get some rest.

"Please, Molly," he whispered. "I need you to get better." He reached over to give her a kiss and quietly closed the door on his way out. Molly stayed in the hospital for three weeks.

"Your mommy is sick and they had to take her to the hospital," Sophie explained to Maggie that afternoon. "This means she will get help and get better. Your daddy went to be with her, so I'll stay with you tonight."

Maggie sat in Sophie's lap and cried. How she longed for a normal happy family and childhood! She sure hoped Sophie was right, but she didn't know what to believe anymore. Suddenly, she jumped up and went to watch television.

"I don't want to talk about it," she stated emphatically. "Tomorrow everything will be okay again."

Sophie knew the child was in pain, but didn't know how to reach her. She suspected abuse, but had no proof, and kept praying she was wrong. Sophie loved the Stelsons very much. This was her third year working for them, and she felt like part of the family.

They are all wonderful people. If only they could talk to each other and share feelings. They are all full of hurt and anger - but won't admit it. I wish there was something I could do, before they destroy all they have.

Absorbed in thought, she walked upstairs to get some things together for Molly and stopped short. The door was ajar and she could see Maggie curled up on Molly's bed, sobbing. Quietly she entered the room and gently took Maggie into her arms. She began to rock her. Maggie clung tight and wept. Sophie did the same.

"I'm Linda Terrio and I'm here to help you."

Molly opened her eyes to see a young woman who was obviously a doctor. She wore a white coat over a pretty yellow blouse and navy skirt. The combination went well with her dark hair and olive complexion. Molly figured she was either Italian or Spanish.

"No one can help me," Molly moaned. "Are you a shrink or something?"

Linda picked up the plea for help in Molly's voice as she answered, "I am a psychologist, and I can try to help you- but you must want to help yourself. I take your attempted suicide to mean a call for help. Do you want to try?"

"Yes," Molly whispered. "I am sick. Please help me."

"Okay, I'll start seeing you in the morning. Tonight, get some sleep, and try not to think about where you are, or why. Tomorrow will be soon enough for that," Ms. Terrio ordered.

For the next three weeks Molly talked and cried as she never had before.

"We'd like to discharge you, tomorrow," Dr. Samson smiled at her. "You've come a long way these past three weeks."

"It'll take time, but I believe you can get better," Linda piped in from behind him. "I have recommended to Wayne that you be sent home, but with some stipulations. I want to see you as an out-patient once a week, and I want to recommend a treatment center in Rochester. I want you to go there four times a year, a week at a time. I'll tell you more about it when I meet with you."

"If you're willing to agree to these terms I'll sign your release papers immediately," the physician said. He had worked along with Linda for some time now and trusted her judgment implicitly.

"I agree and I mean it." The sincerity in Molly's voice came through loud and clear. "I really do want to get better and I'll do whatever it takes."

Chapter Seven

She'll never follow those instructions.

Jake was mulling over the words Dr. Samson had told him a few minutes before. He had come to take his wife home, but first met with the doctor and a lovely young woman whom he soon found was the psychologist assigned to Molly.

"We have explained these instructions to Molly and she has agreed to our terms. It's because of that we're sending her home. Linda has stressed to her that no one can make her better except herself. It'll be difficult, but you must stand back and not try to do for her. It won't happen overnight, but the results will be positive as long as she follows the rules," explained the doctor.

Jake just nodded his head, trying to believe there was still hope. The past three weeks had been torturous for him.

Each day he came to see Molly, and each day she pushed him father away.

She would constantly use such phrases as, "Get out!" "I don't want to see you!" and a few others, which Jake preferred to forget.

Dr. Samson kept assuring Jake that it was her not him. His presence probably made her remember things she'd rather forget. He explained to Jake that he had assigned a psychologist, one of the best, to Molly's case. "She sees Molly every day and this will help. Please, be patient. These outbursts will soon pass and she will want to see you. Maybe it would be better if you would stay away for now."

Despite the doctor's reassurance, Jake always left the hospital feeling alone and hurt.

Now he was here to take her home. He entered the elevator with many mixed feelings. When the doors opened on the third floor, he found for a minute that he could not move.

"Excuse me," came an exasperated voice behind him.

"Oh, sorry," he mumbled to the man trying to get out and quickly stepped out on to the ward.

"Mr. Stelson." He stopped when he heard his name. Turning, he spotted a pretty blond nurse hurrying to catch up to him. "I have your wife's discharge papers ready for you to sign. She's dressed and waiting for you. She's very nervous about going home."

Jake walked back to the desk with Nurse Payne, signed the necessary papers and started back to his wife's room.

Molly looked pretty in her peach blouse and navy slacks. She even had a little make-up on and her hair was styled nicely. She had a small smile on her face, which appeared to Jake to be forced.

He leaned over and gave her a light kiss on the cheek. It was the first time in a long time she did not pull away from him. *Maybe the doctor is right*, he thought, *Maybe there is hope*.

He walked ahead to catch the elevator while the nurse pushed Molly in a wheelchair. "Hospital policy," she said. "We give valet service right to the door."

Sophie was standing on the porch with Maggie when the car pulled up. As soon as it stopped, Maggie let go of Sophie and flew down the stairs. She pulled open her mother's door and dove into her arms. "Momma, I missed you," said the excited six year old. "Please don't go away again - promise?"

Molly didn't respond as she got out of the car and walked slowly up to the house.

"Welcome home, Ms. Stelson." Sophie met her halfway and walked with her to the house. "I've fixed a nice dinner in honor of your return, and Maggie set the table extra pretty tonight."

"I even made you a special place mat, Mom. It says 'welcome home'. Wait till you see it."

A pall came over the room when Molly said she was just too tired to eat and wanted to go straight to her room.

"I'll see your place mat tomorrow, sweetie." She took Maggie's chin lovingly in her hand. "I promise."

Maggie tried to be brave as she nodded her assent, but tears had filled her six-year old eyes. Sophie said nothing and quietly walked to the kitchen, knowing how disappointed Maggie was. Jake silently carried the bags and set them down in Molly's room.

"Maggie has been planning this night for a week now," he chided gently as Molly entered the room. "All the child talked about was Mommy's coming home. We need to do something special. Can't you at least come and sit with us, have - coffee or something?"

"Jake, I can't. You don't know what I've been through. Try to understand how I feel," she whined.

Jake walked out of the room thinking that things would never change.

Tears streamed down Molly's face as she got undressed and climbed into bed. *I know he thinks I'm being selfish. I want to go down stairs more than anything. But I'm scared; really scared. Oh Maggie, I am so sorry, sweetheart,* she whispered to herself. *I hope someday you'll understand. Mommy's trying to get well - honest she is.*

Once under the covers, she rolled over and drifted into a fitful sleep.

After supper, Jake sent Sophie home earlier than usual and put Maggie to bed himself. An hour later, as he left her, he could still hear her sobbing. Heading toward his own room, he could not help but berate himself. "I can't help what I do," he whined, "It's all Molly's fault. She could try and get well. I need love, too."

Maggie held tight to Pandy and sobbed. Her daddy had gone into her room a lot while Molly was away. Each time while he was touching her, Maggie would think, *Mommy will be home soon. She'll help.* Tonight, however, her mother had deserted her and simply went to bed. How could she tell Mom how bad she felt, or what Dad was doing to her?

She had heard his voice at the door and cringed with fear. "How's my big girl doing? Daddy sure needs his baby's love tonight," he said.

She began to cry the minute he touched her. He did something this time he had never done before, and all she knew was that it hurt awful bad. *Why, daddy?* she thought. *Why do you have to hurt me?*

When he left, she sobbed quietly into her pillow and wished she could just disappear - then no one could hurt her again.

Maggie had also hoped to tell her mom about the school Christmas show she was chosen to be in, and explain that rehearsals started next week, after Thanksgiving. Since her Mom didn't come to supper, all her plans had been ruined. Maggie cried herself to sleep, feeling sad and lonely, and in her mind no one seemed to care.

She awoke the next morning with no recollection of the night before. She was becoming an expert at forgetting and being what she thought everyone wanted her to be.

The following January, Molly made her first visit to the private convalescent home/clinic in Rochester. It was not a nursing home, but a refuge for people with mental or emotional problems to learn to cope.

The building was new and modern. It had three separate wings. One wing was for people with drug or alcohol addictions who needed intense help. Another was for folks who had nervous breakdowns and other disorders where they had to stay for a long while, and then there was a wing for people like Molly, who needed to come for a week at a time, when things got too tough for them to handle alone.

Since that day she had visited three other times just as she had told Dr. Samson and Linda she would. Now, over two years later, she continued to come as directed. Even though she still spent much of her time at home in bed, she felt she was continually making progress, and was pleased with herself. Her only concern was being away from Maggie, who was going on eight years old in a few short weeks.

Sophie's there. She'll watch out for her. Molly tried to console herself each time she boarded the bus.

Jake didn't understand his wife's need to come here at all."You always have to think of yourself first, don't you? What about your daughter and your husband? How can you be so selfish?

You're not getting better. You're just avoiding any responsibility."

I'm sorry, Jake. The tears rolled down her cheeks as the bus rolled along the freeway. The guilt feelings would stay with her until her first meeting with her "shrink" in the morning. *I'm doing this for you and Maggie. Can't you see that?*

"Someday he will. Give it time," Linda would say to her. "He's hurting also. Give him time," Linda kept encouraging and reassuring Molly.

"You're making great strides, Mol. I know you sometimes don't think so, but it's true. You're into your third year, and I'm going to challenge you to try talking to Jake. I want you to eat meals with your family at least three nights each week. Do you think you can do it?"

Molly wasn't sure, but agreed to try it. Linda's confidence in her seemed to give Molly the strength to attempt the challenge, even though the idea scared her to death.

Two days later, Molly whistled as she packed. She knew going home this time would be different, and smiled as she thought of the surprise and joy on Jake's and Maggie's faces when she arrived home.

I love you both. I promise things will be different from now on. She grinned from ear to ear as she sat alone on the bench waiting for the afternoon bus.

Chapter Eight

The title this week was *My Most Memorable Experience*, and Maggie was stumped. She sat chewing on her pencil for the longest time trying to think of what to write. Only one idea came and she couldn't possibly use it. What could she write? How could she please her wonderful third grade teacher?

Maggie loved Miss Frazier and would do anything for her. Her beloved teacher was young, very pretty, and extremely creative. Everything she did was fun, and all the kids seemed to like her. She never raised her voice or insulted anyone. The thing Maggie loved best was that everyone was the teacher's favorite, and she encouraged her students to be the best they could be.

Miss. F., as the class lovingly called her, was fair, but could be very stern when the situation warranted it. There were two boys in particular who always picked on the girls. Maggie had become their favorite target, or at least it seemed so to her. But in Miss Frazier's room they were on their best behavior. Maggie felt safe in third grade, and knew that Miss Frazier was her ally and friend.

First grade had been okay. She was always quiet and had a hard time making friends. However, she had learned to read and write that year. Books became her best friends.

"She's always alone," her teacher told her dad at one of the conferences. "Some of the kids think she doesn't like them, so they stay away from her. She seems to be in her own little world."

"That's just Maggie," he responded." She'll snap out of it by next year."

However, second grade came, and things got even worse. In second grade, Maggie tended to be alone most of the time. She had no friends and even her teacher didn't seem to like her.

"Margaret, you are hopeless," her teacher told her when she asked for the directions again. "If you would listen, instead of your constant daydreaming, you'd know what to do. What are you thinking about anyway - boys?"

All the kids laughed at her teacher's teasing, and Maggie fought back the tears and looked down.

"Betty, tell her how to do the paper," Mrs. Rust said to the girl beside her. She threw up her hands and returned to helping Mary, who seemed to be her favorite.

Maggie hated to be called on and never volunteered an answer because she couldn't stand the kids' laughter. She would sit in her seat quietly and hope Mrs. Rust would leave her alone. She was always the butt of jokes and teasing, but neither her teacher nor her parents seemed to care.

"They only tease you because they like you," her mother would tell her.

"Oh, Maggie, for heaven's sake, stop whining," her dad would brush her off. "Kids are like that. Just ignore them."

Maggie spent the whole year alone, trying not to let the teasing hurt her.

At home things were not much better. Her mom still stayed in her room a lot. Often into the night she'd hear dad arguing with mom. Then he would come to her room, and hurt her again and again.

Three times a year mom would go away for a week at a time, and no one would tell her why. "Where did Mommy go?" she innocently asked her dad the first couple of times. "Why did she leave us?"

"Don't ask me," he would snap. "Your mom is crazy, that's all."

Maggie didn't like him saying Mommy was crazy. She knew Mommy was sick, but Daddy didn't seem to care. Why was he so mad at her mother?

70

One day she asked Sophie, who told her it was too hard for her to understand right now. "Wait until you're older."

How Maggie hated those words. There were too many secrets in this house. Maggie soon learned to stop asking and just accepted things. She would wonder sometimes if it was normal for families not to talk about things, to have so many secrets.

Molly went away again in July, and Maggie knew better than to ask.

Maggie was eight years old then and hated being alive. A miracle happened. She entered third grade.

Third grade was so different, and Mags had come to feel more at ease. She was even daring to feel happy and attempted to answer questions. More than anything in the world, she wanted Miss Frazier to like her.

"Twenty more minutes before lunch." Miss Frazier's voice startled her.

I need to think of something, she thought. *But what?*

Every Friday morning they had to write a story. Many of the kids hated this, but not Maggie. She could put anything she wanted on paper and no one had to see it. She even had a secret notebook at home that she wrote in at night. She especially liked it when the class had to make-believe and use their imagination. She preferred to write about what she wished, not what was real.

However, the one experience that kept coming in to her head happened two and a half years before, but she could never write about it. She thought she had forgotten all about it.

Maybe she remembered it now because she wondered if Miss Frazier would believe her story and make it stop. No, she could not get her pencil to move. She had forgotten how to trust any adult, even Miss Frazier.

Two years ago, a week before her sixth birthday, Maggie had just finished her bath and curled up in her bed waiting for Sophie, who had promised to read her a story. She couldn't wait for school to start, so she could learn to read for herself. She wanted so badly to read about far away places and people. Sophie always had a book with her, and shared her enthusiasm for books by reading to Maggie. Sophie's stories always had people who loved their kids and had happy endings. How Maggie wished she could be Cinderella or Sleeping Beauty! Then a handsome prince would come and take her away from here.

Molly had just come home from the hospital and was in bed. Maggie was feeling sad and knew a story would make her feel better. Sophie would pick a happy one for sure. A few minutes later, Sophie came in with a new book, *Charlotte's Web*. No sooner had she opened the book, when Jake walked in.

"Sophie, why don't you head home early tonight? You look exhausted, and I can read to Maggie if you like. Oh, *Charlotte's Web* - one of my favorites."

"Thank you; I'd appreciate that," Sophie answered, "I'm very tired. It's been a long day."

Bending over to kiss Maggie, she whispered, "Good night, Goofy. Be good. I'll see you tomorrow." When she heard the front door close, Maggie began to cry. She didn't make a sound, but large tears rolled out of her eyes and down her cheeks, dripping off her chin like raindrops.

"Daddy please, don't hurt me. I promise I'll be good. I want to go to sleep. Daddy, please."

Jake seemed oblivious to her pleas as he closed the door and came over to her bed. After a particularly bad day at work and home, he felt he needed love and understanding. Totally oblivious to his daughter's needs, he laid down beside her and held her in his arms.

"It's okay, sweetie - Daddy loves you," he said, kissing her. "Can't you love Daddy just a little bit? That's my good girl."

Suddenly, he pulled up her nightie as usual, and started caressing her again. In her mind, Maggie became a beautiful little star whom everybody loved and wanted to enjoy. She tried not to feel his hands and hoped he would stop soon. Then he did something different: he took off his clothes, right in front of her. She tried to pull away, but he held her tight. Then the tears flowed as he... he...

A gentle tap on the shoulder brought her back, and Maggie looked up into Miss Frazier's kind eyes.

"Sweetheart, are you okay?" She sounded concerned. "Do you feel sick?"

Maggie suddenly realized she was crying, and tried to stop, but couldn't. Embarrassed, she looked around and saw that except for her teacher, she was alone in the room. She put her head on her desk and sobbed. It was as if a dam had broken inside of her. She couldn't stop. All the pain in her little body just came gushing out.

Catherine Frazier held Maggie close and let her cry. It was fifteen minutes before Maggie calmed down a little bit, and Catherine tried to talk to her again.

"The other kids went with Mr. Jordan's fourth grade class. They're at lunch. How can I help you, Maggie?" she said quietly. "I know your mom is away. Do you miss her? Want me to call your dad?"

"No!" Maggie didn't mean to yell, then more controlled, she added, "No I'm okay. I just don't feel too good, but I'll be okay. Honest."

Miss Frazier took her into the teacher's lounge and let her lay on the couch. When she returned with a warm cloth to wipe the child's face, she noted to her surprise that Maggie was asleep.

After intercepting the other teachers and offering her classroom to them so they could eat, she hurried downstairs to Mrs. Kenning's office.

Mrs. Grace Kenning had been a teacher and then principal of the school for almost twenty-five years. She knew many of the families in town. In fact, Grace had taught quite a few of the parents of the present students. Maybe she could shed some light regarding Maggie Stelson. After all, Chaffee wasn't that big.

Mrs. Kenning's long-time assistant informed Catherine that Grace was on the phone if she wished to wait. Catherine groaned, as she knew that when her boss got on the phone it could be a while. She flopped down in the empty chair expecting to be there for quite a while. Beside her sat a mother and daughter. The little

73

girl had bright red hair and freckles, and looked like she might be old enough for first or second grade. Catherine wondered if the child was a new student. Miss Frazier smiled at her, and said hello to her and her mother, then sat back to wait.

Twenty minutes later, Catherine was getting up to leave since her class would be coming in from recess shortly, when the assistant noted that the principal was finally off the phone.

Mrs. Kenning opened her office door. She had a radiant smile which seemed to stay, no matter what problems she had to face. Grace was close to sixty, but looked years younger. She had lovely white hair which she kept short with soft curls, and she always dressed impeccably.

She was kind and loving, and knew every student in the school by name. Every morning she'd be out at the door to greet them, give out hugs and listen to stories. The children absolutely adored her. They hated being sent to her when they did something wrong. They weren't so much afraid of being punished as much as having her be disappointed in them.

Mrs. Frazier liked working for her, and knew the other teachers felt the same. Mrs. Kenning was in her element as principal. She was a natural.

"Catherine, hi. Is there something I can help you with?" Grace asked, surprised to see her there.

"I'd like to talk with you about one of my students, but I know these folks are waiting to see you now. Besides, I have to pick up my class from recess, but in ten minutes they go to music and I have a free period. Could we talk then?"

" Of course. I'll find you as soon as I finish here," she smiled. "If it develops into something serious, feel free to interrupt."

Catherine left the office relieved. She knew Grace was true to her word, and was confident she could help, or would at least make every effort. She took a minute to check on Maggie, who was still asleep, and went to pick up her students. After dropping them at music, she went to get some paper work done before Mrs. Kenning came by.

Catherine could not focus on the tests she had to grade, as her mind kept drifting back to Maggie.

Darling, I know you are unhappy and lonely, she thought, *how can I reach you, how can I help you?* She put her head down and cried for her student whom she saw withdraw a little more every day.

Catherine jumped with a start when she heard the knock at her door. Sure it was Grace, she quickly wiped her eyes and yelled to her to come in.

"I was just grading some papers," she said, without looking up. "I'm just about done."

"Miss Frazier, this is Rose Arlton and her mother Denise. They recently moved to Chaffee, and Rose will be entering your class."

"How do you do?" Catherine shook hands with Denise. Then she turned to her new pupil and smiled. "Welcome, Rose. I am sure you'll be very happy here. You'll make number twenty six in our class, and I believe we'll now have an equal number of boys and girls."

"Rose will be starting on Monday," noted Grace. "They need to go, but I insisted we at least say hello. I'll walk them to the door and then come back up for our meeting."

"Fine," smiled Catherine, still a bit taken aback. Rose was small for her age, and Catherine figured her for first or second grade. "Oh well, I guess I need to give up my supply desk," she said to herself. There was one extra student desk in the room, so she kept supplies, in it and the kids helped themselves if they needed to. She'd just have to find a different location and scanned the room for possibilities.

Grace was back in no time, and they began to discuss Maggie's situation at length. It wasn't long before they came up with a possible solution. They decided to give Maggie the job of showing Rose around. It would make her feel important and special, and hopefully get her a friend. Catherine admitted to Grace that Maggie was very much a loner.

"Maggie is a good student and hard worker, but she keeps very much to herself. I believe the other children tease her a lot, though

she never says anything. I put a stop to it immediately if I catch
them. She seems very distant and shy, as if there is something
inside of her which is hurting. I believe this because even when she
smiles, her eyes are always sad."

"Well, let's give our idea a try. Maybe it will be just the ticket
to bring Maggie out of herself. If this doesn't work, I'll set up a
meeting with her parents. I know there are pressures at home and
don't want to be too hasty in adding another one. I'll get your class
from Music, and you wake Maggie. I'm sure things will be okay.
Let's keep our fingers crossed."

Maggie was quiet the rest of the afternoon, and during free
time read a book at her desk. Her eyes were puffy and red when she
came back to the room, but none of the other children had noticed.
They left her alone and went about their activities.

Catherine had the class pick up a little earlier than usual and
when they were all back in their seats, she told them about Rose.

"Class, we will be getting a new student in our room on
Monday. Her name is Rose Arlton, and she and her family just
moved into town. I have decided to appoint Maggie Stelson as
ambassador to show Rose around and help her out with anything
she needs to know."

There were a few snickers from one side of the room, but a look
from the teacher was enough to make the guilty ones stop. Maggie
sat in silence as usual, yet Catherine was sure she saw a new spark
in those sad brown eyes.

"Class is dismissed. Get your things and walk quietly to you
busses."

When the line was on its way, Catherine turned to get her own
things together and almost tripped over Maggie.

"Sweetheart, you'll miss your bus," she said kindly.

Maggie looked up at her. "Thank you," she spoke in a barely
audible tone. Before Catherine could acknowledge her remark,
Maggie dashed out of the room and down the hall toward her bus.

Catherine smiled and crossed her fingers.

Chapter Nine

Monday morning Maggie was up and practically dressed when Molly went to wake her. Lately Molly had been trying very hard to be there for Maggie in the mornings. She was surprised to find her daughter awake. Maggie was not a morning person and sometimes it took much effort and coaxing to get her up.

"Is there a party today or something?" Molly queried. The child was definitely excited about something.

"There's a new girl at school and I got picked to be ambassador to show her around."

"Do you think you can do that? I mean, you've always been so shy. Why did she pick you?"

Maggie tried to hide her disappointment over her mother's words. *Why can't anyone like me?* she thought as she walked downstairs. *What is so wrong with me?*

Riding the bus, she began to have second thoughts. Maybe her mother was right. Maybe she couldn't do it. What if she did something wrong and everyone laughed?

By the time the vehicle reached school, she had decided to tell Mrs. Frazier she'd rather not do it.

Before Maggie had a chance to voice her decision, Mrs. Frazier began to speak. "Maggie, this is Rose Marie Arlton. She will be joining our class this year. Her family just moved here from Augusta, Georgia. Rose, this is Maggie Stelson. She is to be our class ambassador for the week. Do you know what that means?"

"No, Ma'am," Rose said as she greeted Maggie. "Hi," Rose said cheerfully, "I'm eight, at least until January, then I'll be nine. Are you eight also? I hope we can be friends. Where do you live? We bought a house on Elm Street. How boring, but it's easy to spell."

"Hi," Maggie said shyly, "I live on Ellsworth Avenue. I don't know where Elm Street is." She spoke quietly and awkwardly.

Catherine watched them with a smile, and knew that somehow this would help Maggie.

Catherine had driven home Friday admiring Mrs. Kenning even more, and praying their plan would work. Now she was seeing the tiniest of smiles as Maggie showed Rose where to put her coat and bag. From that day on, the girls were inseparable.

Rose was full of energy, enthusiasm, and mischief. She loved to laugh and have fun and she was bringing Maggie out of herself a little more each day. It had been two months since she had introduced the children, and Catherine was seeing great improvement in Maggie. In fact, one day in November, she had to send the two of them to the office for talking during a test. Grace told her later, "I had to be stern, but wanted to congratulate Maggie for the offense."

Only she and Catherine would ever understand her remark.

"Rose invited me to spend the night, tonight. Can I go? " Maggie asked her parents during dinner.

Molly was doing much better, and came to dinner almost every night. Her setbacks and "attacks" were less often, less severe and she was happier. Jake was glad to have her back, but conversations were still a bit awkward at times. He almost never came to Maggie's room at night, and she was beginning to forget.

"I don't see why not," said Molly. "It is the weekend. What do you think, Jake?"

"Huh?" he was startled when she touched his arm. "I'm sorry, dear - what did you say?"

"Maggie wants to go to Rose's overnight. I thought it would be okay. What do you think?"

"Yeah, sure, fine with me," he stammered. Then he quickly added, "Maybe if it's okay with Rose's folks, she could stay for the weekend. That would give us some time alone, and I think we need to talk. Why don't you call and ask them, Maggie?" her dad suggested.

She ran from the room and immediately dialed her friend's number. Molly felt elated. She had been waiting for him to want this time alone with her, and her patience had paid off. Hopefully they could begin to get things back to the way they were before.

"Yes, Jake," she spoke to herself. "I have so much to say to you too. I am ready to make us a real family again. "

Jake trembled inside. I know she wants us to make up and start again. *I just have to tell her about Juliann. This weekend will be the opportunity I have been waiting for.*

"They said it was fine and I could come over anytime. I'll pack right away. Will you drive me over, Dad?"

An hour later she was sitting in Rose's room confiding to her friend.

"I just know they're going to make up and we'll be a real family again. I can't wait."

Rose smiled at her friend's excitement and nodded in agreement.

Rose was a small wiry girl,with beautiful red hair that hung about two inches below her shoulders. Her green eyes sparkled all the time, and her round cheery face was covered with a blanket of freckles. She was small for her age, and came to about Maggie's chin. She was very bright, imaginative, and did very well in school. Her dad had told her she'd be the perfect student except for the fact that she talked too much. Her report cards always had "needs improvement" under conduct.

"I guess it just proves you're an Arlton," Dad would wink at her after scolding her and warning to try harder. Then he'd smile and send her on her way.

The Arlton's were a lively bunch, and Maggie never knew what to expect when she came for a visit. She loved coming here; they were becoming her second family. In fact, one time Mrs. Arlton had taken her, Rose, and Rose's two sisters to the movies and asked for one adult ticket and four children's tickets for her "four" daughters. Maggie was flattered and grinned about it for days afterward.

Rose had two sisters and two brothers, and she was right smack in the middle. Her dad had worked in a nursery down south, as he loved plants and flowers. For as long as Rose remembered he had dreamed of opening a nursery of his own. When he hurt his back last year, he had to move inside to handle sales and services, rather than trees and shrubs. Then a long time friend wrote to him from Buffalo, and asked him to become a partner in his new endeavor. Fred Arlton jumped at the chance, and was now half owner of The Flower Bed.

They sold everything from tropical plants, floral bouquets, small indoor trees, and shrubs. Fred came home after the first month and stated at supper, "Business is really blossoming. Our shop has taken root." Everyone laughed at his puns, and after her very loud groan, his wife Denise went over and gave him a hug.

"I'm so happy for you, dear. You've waited so long." She was so proud of, and so in love with her husband.

They'd been married twelve years and struggled hard for the first two years. He did odd jobs in landscaping until he landed a job with Blakley's Nursery in Thomson, about twenty miles from their home in Augusta, a well- established and well-patronized business. Fred was in charge of the green house plants and shrubs, a very lucrative position, though it didn't sound that way. He loved his work and took great pride in his plants and flowers. He was a hard worker, a good provider, and Denise, his first and only love, loved him dearly.

"My dad waters flowers all day," Rose announced one time in kindergarten. The following Saturday, Fred took her with him and showed her all he did.

Denise worked full time in the library until she had her first child, then only part time. She quit all together when her second son was born. Now she did some volunteering on Saturday afternoons at the library reading stories and playing games with varying groups of children.

By the time Rose was born, Denise had become a great mother, and loved every minute of it. She was a natural with kids and as hers got older the house always seemed to be full of them.

She had two more girls after Rose, and would've loved to have had more, but after Iris, now four, Denise developed ovarian cancer, and had to have a hysterectomy. For the first eighteen months of Iris' life, Denise was in and out of the hospital receiving chemotherapy. She used to say she wanted her baby to look like her. "Since she is taking too long to grow hair, I'll just have to let mine fall out," she'd laugh.

"She's okay now," Rose was telling Maggie about her mom's illness. "Now her hair is all grown back and she's not throwing up all the time. But she can't have anymore kids."

Maggie was awed by Rose's candid description of her mother's cancer. At home, she was always told not to tell people her mother was sick.

"It's no one else's business," Dad would tell her. "Just tell people she is very busy and can't get out as much."

He got mad at her when she suggested that it was a lie.

"It's only a white lie. Sometimes it's better to tell a white lie than give out information to people who could use it against you."

Maggie never understood what he meant, but knew he would be very angry if she told, so she just kept quiet.

Now, Maggie ventured to tell Rose everything about her family. To her pleasant surprise and relief, Rose still liked her and wanted to be her friend. Rose never told a soul about Maggie's secret.

Besides Iris, Rose's youngest sister, she had a sister Lily who was two years younger than she and two brothers, Elmer and Ashley. Being a florist, Fred thought it would be fun to name his kids after flowers and trees. When Ashley, the oldest boy, five years Rose's senior, was born, Fred's idea didn't seem too ludicrous.

81

However, two years later when they had their second son, Denise balked.

"But Elmer is such an awful name," she groaned. "Everyone will tease him as he grows up."

"He'll be distinguished," Fred argued the point. "But if you insist we can call him Bob. After all, his middle name is Robert."

So Elmer Robert was the name he was given.

About six months later, Ashley solved the problem. He was learning to talk, and instead of Bob he was saying Bud. Fred laughed when he heard it.

"Bud - that's a great nickname. After all, he's a small son of a florist, isn't he?"

Now at age eleven, Bud was growing to be quite handsome and though she'd die if anyone knew, Maggie was really smitten by him.

Jake waited until Maggie was let into the house before he drove off. He could hear the loud laughter and cheers even in the car, when the door was opened.

Maggie seems so much happier lately, he thought as he drove home. *Rose and her family have been just the thing for her. God knows she hasn't had much of a childhood with us.*

He wanted to blame Molly for that, but knew he was just as responsible for his daughters' loneliness. It was as if she lived in her own little world all the time. She was constantly in front of the TV, and spoke of the characters as if they were real. Up until this year, she had been living a fantasy.

Last September, when he left to drive to Rochester to pick up Molly, he had tried to convince Maggie to come along.

"No," she said adamantly, "It's time for Gilligan. Last night the Professor thought they would be rescued tonight. I need to watch and see if it happens."

He left the house bewildered, and feeling as if he and Molly had been replaced by TV as Maggie's reality. What he didn't realize, or want to believe, was that he had hit the nail right on the head.

Other times, she'd come in breathless from school, throw her books down, and turn on the tube. She'd get so engrossed in her "programs" that she wouldn't hear Sophie telling her to pick up her things or change her clothes.

One day, Sophie had had enough, and turned off the TV. Maggie went into a rage, screaming and kicking for an hour. When Jake arrived home he found her sobbing in a corner, still in her school clothes. Her books and papers were torn and scattered all over the room. Deaf to Sophie's argument that she was using her behavior to be manipulative and should be punished, Jake let her go back to watching TV.

"She'll pick up later when the show's over, won't you sweetie?" He tried to appease Sophie. "She's only a little girl."

Sophie threw up her hands and went back to the kitchen. She never interfered again.

Jake drove home in silence, wondering how he was going to tell Molly about Juli. Was it fair to her and Maggie? Lately, she was getting better, and Maggie was coming out of her shell. What if his love for Juli pushed them both back into their own little worlds again? Yet he had to think of himself and his happiness. Didn't he?

Chapter Ten

Jake had never meant to fall in love with Juliann. After all, she was probably fifteen years older than he was, and worked for him. Yet, slowly over the last two years, it happened. Maybe he wanted it to happen.

He had been so lonely since Maggie was born. He deserved love and happiness as well as anyone else.

"I didn't plan it. It just happened," he shouted to Molly over her tears. "You were always so sick and never cared about me. Juli was always there to listen. I was comfortable with her. She was a good friend and confidant. Molly, she covered for me many times when I rushed home to care for you. Everyday she'd ask me how you were doing. She wasn't trying to break up our marriage." His pleading was falling on deaf ears.

"Yeah, right," she choked through her tears.

"All those long hours at the office, those *projects*. I should have guessed. Were you sleeping with her while I was home sick?" Her sarcasm was biting, and Jake could no longer hold his temper.

"I stood by you all that time, whether you chose to believe it or not. I would go to the office because I couldn't take your tantrums and self -pity anymore. Juliann was a listening ear, a comforting friend, and nothing more!

"Do you want to know when things changed? Fine - I'll tell you! It was during those three weeks you were in the hospital after your last suicide attempt. I just couldn't take anymore. Every time I went to visit you, you'd push me away. You told me you hated me, that I was insensitive and didn't care. You treated me like shit.

Finally, Doctor Samson told me it may be better if I stayed away. He said, and I quote, 'Maybe you are reminding her of things she's not ready to face yet.'

"So I left. Where was I supposed to go? Your folks had taken Maggie, and Sophie took some vacation time, and I hated going home.

By now Molly was sitting on the bed sniffling, just staring. She had never seen Jake like this, and she didn't know what to say. He had paused for a moment awaiting her response, but since she gave no comment, he continued.

"That day your good ol' doctor basically told me to get lost, I went back to the office. I tried to work, but couldn't focus. No, Juliann was not there, if that's what you're thinking. However, she came in a while later. I only knew because I felt a gentle hand on my shoulder. I was sobbing then and out of control.

Suddenly, she spoke as if she were my mother.

"What you need is a shower, a good home cooked meal, and a good night's sleep. I am driving you home. I will pick you up in the morning and you can get your car then. Don't try to argue. Let's go."

"I followed her like a whipped puppy. When we got home, she went right to the kitchen, and sent me upstairs to shower and change.

"Molly, we laughed and talked as we ate a simple meal of spaghetti and salad. She listened to stories of my childhood, laughed at my jokes, and helped me forget my pain. When she left, the house seemed even more empty. True to her word, she picked me up for work and we drove the twenty miles to Buffalo, smiling and happy. I hadn't felt that way in a long time.

"At two o'clock, she announced she was leaving work early. 'Give me your house key,' she said. I looked perplexed but before I could speak she grinned slyly, 'Don't argue, just do it.' I said, 'Yes Ma'am,' and tossed her the key.

"When I arrived home, the lights were on, and the place was beckoning. I entered through the front door to smells so wonderful they made my mouth water.

'You go get cleaned up,' she shouted from the kitchen, 'dinner is almost ready.' I took the stairs as if I had wings, and actually sang in the shower. The giddiness I felt was so freeing, and by the time I wandered downstairs, she had a scrumptious fish dinner all laid out. She stayed quite late that night, talking and laughing. I tried to get her to stay the night, but she refused. I hated to see her go.

"From then on this became our routine each night. By the middle of the second week, I convinced her to stay over.

"While she drove home, I told myself I was being absurd. 'You are a married man, and in love with that older woman.'

"Since you've come home, we have been seeing each other at least twice a week. Those evenings I work late I am actually with her.

"I'm sorry, Molly. I don't want to hurt you, but I can't go on this way. I have wanted to tell you for sometime, but couldn't find the right time or the right words. I'll pack my things and move out before Maggie comes home, unless you'd rather have me stay and be the one to tell her."

Molly was in a state of shock. Things were going so much better, or so she thought. How could she have been so stupid? Why couldn't she see? How she wished she could talk to Linda.

"Molly?" Jake spoke gently.

"Go," she said quietly. "Just go."

When she heard the door close, she sobbed. When she couldn't cry anymore, Molly started to dial Linda's number. Then after a brief hesitation, she hung up the phone, picked it up again and called Pat.

Chapter Eleven

"Maggie, your mom just drove up," Bud yelled.

"We're coming," the girls called in unison from Rose's bedroom. A minute later they came giggling down the stairs, Maggie's bag in hand.

"Thank you so much for everything, Mrs. Arlton." Maggie gave her adopted mother a big hug. So often she wished this woman truly was her mother and she was part of this happy family. Still, maybe going home today would be different. After all, she stayed overnight so her parents could talk.

"Everything will work out, now," she had told Rose the night before as they lay in bed. "You'll see - we'll be a real family again." Her voice sounded like she was trying to convince herself as well as her best friend.

Rose hugged her friend and answered, "I sure hope so. You deserve it."

After saying her goodbyes to the rest of the family, Maggie skipped down the walk in anticipation of great things ahead. Opening the car door, her face fell. Sophie was driving her mom's car. She loved Sophie a great deal but seeing her now, Maggie felt disappointment and rage. The housekeeper's presence said only one thing to Maggie; more trouble.

"What's wrong now?" she asked quietly as she slid into the passenger seat. The fear in her voice was evident. "Is Mommy sick again? Did she have to go away again? What's wrong!?" She began to panic.

"It's okay, sweetie." Sophie put her hand gently on Maggie's arm. "You're mom did not leave. She is a little upset and asked me to come and get you. Auntie Pat is with her now."

"Is there something wrong with Dad then?" she was groping for answers.

Sophie's silence answered her question loud and clear.

"Where's daddy?" Maggie practically yelled. Her eyes were wide, her face drained of all color, and her voice shaky. "What happened to my daddy?"

"Your mom will explain everything, honey," was all Sophie would say.

The rest of the ride was quiet as Sophie drove and Maggie stared out the window, tears rolling down her face. Sophie's heart ached for this special little girl. She had already had so much pain in her life, and she was only nine.

Sophie had just pulled up to the curb when Maggie jumped from the car and ran up to her house. Not even bothering to close the door, the child stormed into the den, where she found her mother and Aunt Pat sitting quietly. Her mom's eyes were puffy red, and her hair was unkempt. Her clothes were wrinkled and disheveled like they had been slept in.

"Maggie, baby," her mom started to reach out to her.

"Where is my daddy?" Maggie screamed at her mother. "What happened *now*? Where is he?" She stamped her foot. "Tell me."

"Darling, your dad left last night," her mother whispered to her. "He just-"

Her child interrupted with an anger that Molly had never seen before.

"What did you do now?" she screamed. "You never liked daddy. All you ever did was fight with him. You had to always be sick and stay in your room. You never cared about us. He was always so sad and wished you would come downstairs with us. But you never would. You're selfish and hateful. You probably made daddy leave! Why couldn't you try to love him and me? I never want to talk to you again. You're not my mother. I hate you. I hate this family and this house. Why does everything always have to be so wrong here?

Why can't we be happy like Rose's family? I wish I was never born. I wish I died like Patty. She was the only daughter you ever wanted anyway. Daddy's lucky because he doesn't have to live here anymore. Don't ever talk to me again! I hate you!" She turned and ran from the room. A minute later, the three women heard her bedroom door slam.

Molly sobbed uncontrollably in Pat's arms while her good friend tried to comfort her.

"She's just angry and hurt. I'm sure she didn't mean those things. Give her time and she'll be okay."

"No," replied Molly. "I *have* been a rotten mother and wife. Everything she said is true. I'm no good. Oh, Pat, what am I going to do?"

Pat feared for her friend as she heard the despair in her voice. She looked up at Sophie, then back to Molly.

Sophie sat on the other side of her boss and placed a comforting hand on her shoulder. "Honey." She spoke gently and softly. "Maybe you should talk to Linda. She can help you more than we can. Would you like me to call her for you?"

Molly's shoulders relaxed a little at the suggestion, and she nodded with relief at Sophie. As the housekeeper got up to make the call, Pat looked at her friend with relief in her eyes. She had been with Molly since last night, but had no idea as how to help except to listen. Sophie's suggestion was a godsend, and Pat wondered why she herself hadn't thought of Linda earlier.

Pat Walsch had rushed over to the Stelson home as soon as she got Molly's heart-wrenching call the previous evening. She had heard the desperation in her young friend's voice, and prayed the whole way there that Molly wouldn't do anything foolish.

"Sophie," she called to her roommate after hanging up the phone. "I'm going to Molly's and will probably stay the night." She filled the woman in as she quickly threw some things into an overnight bag.

"Be careful driving," Sophie yelled from the doorway. "I'll come over in the morning to help."

Over the years, Sophie and Pat had become close friends. The short meetings in the Stelson kitchen when Pat came for a visit began their camaraderie. Soon their little tete a tetes over coffee developed into evenings out, good restaurants and good movies. Eventually a deep friendship developed between the two women.

Then, about two years ago, they were enjoying pasta at a small Italian restaurant when Pat suggested they become roommates.

"Why be two old maids living alone when we can be two old maids living together?" was the way she phrased it.

At first Sophie was taken aback by the proposal, but the more she thought about it, the more she liked the idea. But how could she afford her share of the rent on her salary? Then, as fate would have it, she received the following letter

> *"Dear Ms. Martinez,*
> *I am John Mason, a lawyer, and I*
> *represent your Aunt Lucia. As I am sure you*
> *are aware, your aunt passed away two months*
> *ago in San Antonio, Texas."*

"It's true," she told Pat, to whom she was reading the letter. "I had a phone call from my cousin, Jose. Unfortunately, I couldn't get away at the time. I was heartbroken. Aunt Lucia was like a mother to me and I loved her dearly. I was always at her house growing up. When Uncle Paul got so sick, I helped her take care of him. Jose had moved to Texas, and she had no other relatives near by. The year and a half Paul had cancer, she and I got very close. I bawled for a week when she moved to Texas to live with her son. I knew it was the best thing, but I was heartbroken, and missed her dearly.

"We'd write often, and then for some unknown reasons her letters stopped. It was shortly after that that Jose called to say she had had a stroke and passed away shortly after." A tear rolled down her cheek, and she continued to read the letter:

"   *..I wish to inform you that she has left*
    you a sizable amount of money from her
    estate. Please call me at 1-683-904-2721
    and I will give you further details.
                        Sincerely yours,
              John T. Mason, Attorney-at-law"

After making the call, Sophie returned to the kitchen in stunned silence. She had inherited a *huge* amount of money.

"He has to come to New York in two days for other business, so his firm assigned him to my case. I made an appointment for him to come here on Saturday with the necessary papers. All I need to do is show him positive identification, sign the papers, and the money is mine. He'll have the check with him."

The following week, Sophie put her windfall into a CD account at the advice of her lawyer. She had enough to pay her share of the closing costs on a home, and could probably manage her half of the mortgage payments on the interest alone for many years to come. Needless to say, she had no qualms when she and her new "roomy" closed the deal on their new four-bedroom condominium.

They each were able to have a bedroom, sitting room, and private bath. The condo was a town house and the bottom floor consisted of a large eat-in kitchen, living room with stone fireplace, a small laundry area, and half bath. Upstairs were the bedrooms. They were set up in a way as to have a bathroom between each pair. Both women fell in love with their new home the minute they saw it. It was located on the outskirts of Buffalo, close to the city, but not in the midst of the noise and traffic. Pat had about a ten minute ride to her shop each day. Sophie had to drive about half an hour to get to Chaffee. However, she loved every minute of it. She had bought herself a new car out of her inheritance, a light blue Ford Taurus. It was her pride and joy.

After about ten minutes, Sophie came back in to the room carrying the portable phone.

"Molly, I got a hold of Linda, and she would like to speak to you."

Hesitantly, Molly took the receiver and spoke with the raspy hoarseness of one who had been crying for a good length of time.

"Hello, Linda." She spoke with a quiet sadness.

She said no more for quite a while except "okay". Then Molly blurted out, "But what will I do with Maggie? Okay, okay." She had responded over and over to her mentor on the other end of the line.

"Okay, I will," were her final words, and she hung up.

Molly stared straight ahead and spoke as if she were talking to herself. It was as if she was unaware of the presence of her two friends.

"She wants me to come to Rochester to the clinic for the week. She said it was only a precaution, so I wouldn't have a relapse. She strongly urged me to and wants me to call her back in half an hour with an answer. I want to go," she continued. There was a distance in her voice, a longing. " But how can I leave Maggie now? She can't stay here alone. I don't know what to do."

Pat glanced at her roommate and knew from the look in her eyes that they were in agreement.

"Mol," she began. "Why don't we take Maggie to our place for the week? Either way, Sophie would have to drive out here so she can drive Mags to and from school each day. We both love her, and you can relax and get well. Linda's right - you need the time in Rochester. Please let us help you."

"You two are the best friends I have." Molly turned back to them with relief in her eyes. "I'll go tell Maggie and then call Linda back."

"Tell me what?" They all turned in the direction of the tiny little voice coming from the hallway.

"Tell me what!" she repeated through gritted teeth. She looked so small and vulnerable that Molly could only stare.

"Maggie, darling," Pat said. "How would you like to come and stay with Sophie and me for a while? You've never been to our new place, have you?"

Her eyes filled up, but she refused to let the tears come. "What for?" she asked weakly. " I need to stay here with Mommy."

"Your mom has to go away for a while to get better. It'll only be for a week then things will be better."

"Things will never be better," she choked. There was a despair and hopelessness in her voice. "I'll go pack."

Why doesn't anyone care about me? God, why do they all hate me. I need help, too. I need someone to love me, too. What is wrong with me? These words haunted her all the way to Aunt Patty's and Sophie's house. That night she cried herself to sleep out of sheer loneliness.

Chapter Twelve

Tuesday morning Sophie drove Maggie to school a little early. Leaving the child on the playground, she went inside to explain the situation to Maggie's teacher. They had decided to let Mags sleep in the day before instead of getting her up for school. Sunday night she had fallen asleep later than her normal bed time. She had had an emotional and exhausting day, and a fitful, restless night.

"I finally got her to sleep," Sophie spoke quietly to Pat. She had given her bed to Maggie and went to share Pat's bed for the week. "I think we should forget school tomorrow," she went on. "The kid's been through a lot. She deserves a day to just be pampered." Pat nodded in agreement as she stifled a yawn. "I can get off by noon. Why don't I just come home and three of us can do something really special?"

"What a great idea," exclaimed Sophie. "Maybe the zoo or a movie? I know the carnival is supposed to open tomorrow. Maybe we could go there and ride all the rides?"

Pat laughed at her friend. "I hope Maggie is as excited as you are. Why don't we let her decide?" She reached over to turn out the light before her pal could comment.

"Okay." Sophie lay there and smiled. She loved Pat very much and found her very attractive. She had known for a few years about her lesbianism. So many times she had been tempted to broach the subject with Pat. Maybe this week would prove helpful for their relationship as well as supporting Molly. "You never know," she mumbled to herself, then rolled over and fell into a deep sleep.

Maggie didn't awaken Monday until after eleven. Sophie ran upstairs to the child's cries.

"It's okay," her caretaker said gently. "You're at my house, darling. You're safe."

Maggie held tight to Sophie as she remembered the events that brought her there. She got up and dressed as if she were still asleep. There was no emotion in the little girl's eyes. She looked like a tiny little waif who was going through the motions of living.

Watching her, Sophie wondered if the poor baby had finally been pushed too far. A tear rolled down her face at the frightening thought.

Molly called at noon to say she had arrived safely. Maggie refused to speak to her.

Molly arrived at the clinic Monday morning, and, true to her word, Linda was waiting for her at the receptionist's desk. She walked her patient to her room on the second floor.

"You get settled and relax a bit. After lunch we'll talk."

Molly set her bag on the bed, feeling nothing but gratitude for the woman. Meeting Linda was the best thing that had come out of her attempted suicide years earlier.

Linda Terrio was a certified psychologist, who moved to New York from Pittsburgh shortly before meeting Molly for the first time. After Molly's suicide attempt she was called in as a consultant. She met with Molly daily while she was in Buffalo Memorial Hospital. Following her discharge, Ms. Stelson came once a week to her office.

The recently built home/clinic in Rochester was non-profit and relied on volunteer help. Since Linda volunteered her time every three months, she suggested Molly come at the times she would be there. It would give her a chance for more intense therapy in a new and different environment. The first week, Molly knew Linda was right. She felt safe and peaceful in her room.

Linda had only been a psychologist for five years when her husband was transferred to Buffalo from Pennsylvania. A new branch of Dalton Chemical Company was opening and he was asked to be the new area manager. It meant a substantial raise and job security, so he had jumped at the chance.

The Terrios had been in Buffalo three months when Linda was finally able to find a psychiatrist to hire her. She worked at the office of a well known and respected psychiatrist and loved it. Her case load was growing all the time, as was her reputation. There were times when she felt overwhelmed, trying to juggle work, home, and family, but organizational skills were innate to her, and she was able to schedule her time well. In fact, she actually liked the challenge of working schedules and "making" time.

Linda was a short woman with naturally curly black hair, and lovely, kind, green eyes. She wore silver- rimmed glasses and always had long, dangling earrings.

"They make me feel taller, somehow," she confided to Molly one day when she commented on a particularly long pair.

From the time her Girl Scout troop had planned and carried out a special Christmas party for one of the local personal care homes, Linda had always wanted to help people, so she decided she would become a social worker. However, after her freshman year at the University of Pittsburgh she decided to transfer her major to psychology, believing she could do more as a psychologist.

She believed in keeping abreast of the latest trends and treatments, and was a great believer in John Bradshaw's inner child theories. He lectured often on such topics as "Healing Your Inner Child" and "How to Help the Dysfunctional Family". She had been to all of his workshops, and repeatedly used his books or tapes with her patients.

"I want you to read this book and we'll discuss it at our next session," she was constantly instructing her clients.

She believed the only way her patients would get better was if they were willing to work. Those willing to do the leg work were the ones who made progress and were eventually "cured".

Molly was one of the latter, and Linda was very proud of her progress.

At one- thirty the two women were again sitting together in the familiar office. Molly relaxed as soon as she dropped into the deep leather couch, which to her made the office Linda's.

Molly was relieved to hear Linda say she didn't feel this incident meant failure, only a setback.

"Molly, I am beginning to believe there is something you are not telling me."

"That's not true! I tell you everything!" She was truly angered and hurt by her counselor's remark.

"I'm sorry," Linda quickly responded. "I didn't mean that you were intentionally keeping things from me. I believe there is something bothering you so deep inside that you don't know it. I think you have suppressed all memory of the hurt that I believe is there. I believe it triggers the way you respond to events that occur in your life now and will in the future."

"Oh, I understand," mumbled Molly. She really didn't comprehend any of it.

"Molly," Linda came over and sat beside her on the couch, putting her hand on Molly's leg. "With your permission, I'd like to ask Dr. Strong to help me help you. He has a great deal of experience with helping people remember past events and dealing with them. I believe he can help you. He is extremely qualified and will do nothing to hurt you."

"I-I-I don't know," Molly's voice was practically non- existent. Linda had to strain to hear her. "Will you be with us?"

"Of course, I will. And Molly - he can do nothing unless you give him the okay. Would you like to try?"

"Yes," she said weakly. "When?"

"I'd like to tell him a little about your case up to now, if it's okay with you. He'll be here this evening. I'll talk to him and see if we can set up our first session tonight. Is that okay with you?"

Molly nodded, wondering what she was getting herself into. She trusted Linda implicitly, and knew she wouldn't suggest anything that was not good for her patient. Still, Molly walked back to her room with a feeling of fearful anxiety, wondering what the evening's session would reveal.

In Molly's opinion, Dr. Strong was the perfect name for the man who entered Linda's inner sanctum at five minutes after seven. He had delayed his entrance for those first five minutes so that Linda could help Molly feel at ease. It hadn't worked.

The only word the patient could think of to describe the psychiatrist was gigantic. He was at least six foot four, with the broadest shoulders she had ever seen. He had a paunch beginning to inch over his belt, but still seemed in pretty good physical shape.

His hazel green eyes sparkled under bushy gray eyebrows which matched his long beard and thinning hair. He had eyelashes any woman would kill for, and a very comforting smile. Molly thought that if she had met him in a dark alley, she'd probably die of fright. Yet his ruddy complexion, kind eyes, and gentle smile told her this monster of a man probably caught flies and put them outside rather than kill them. He could never hurt anybody.

"I'm Doctor Strong." He reached out to shake her hand. Her tiny hand looked minuscule in his massive paw as she shook it. "I am here to help you. Will you trust me?"

She nodded quietly and sighed with relief. The hardest work she had ever done began in earnest.

"I want you to lie on the couch," he coaxed, "and just think of the most relaxing place you know. Picture it in you mind. Become a part of it and relax..."

She drifted back in time to a small, secluded space she used to visit often. Suddenly, she was back sitting in her secret place under the big evergreen tree in her front yard. Molly began to remember.

Chapter Thirteen

"What is the matter with you?" Mrs. Harris impatiently asked her daughter, "All you've done since you turned twelve is to whine and be difficult. What happened to the happy, carefree Molly I used to know?"

Molly shrugged her shoulders and left the room. She didn't know how to answer the question.

I don't know, she thought, as she walked outside. *I just don't know how I feel, anymore.*

Suddenly the tears started again and she headed for the refuge of her tree. The large evergreen tree in the front yard had become her secret hiding place three years before. She loved to crawl under the branches and sit among the pine needles, leaning up against the sturdy trunk. Here she could sit and think, or cry, or pray, and nobody could touch her, nobody could find her. Over the years, she had brought a few of her things out there to make the space truly her own, and so far, no one had discovered it. It was hers and hers alone. Here she could relax and feel safe. That afternoon, she automatically crawled under the massive branches and began to sob uncontrollably.

Why are things so mixed up lately? she wondered.

All her emotions were confusing her, and she couldn't tell anyone exactly how she felt. *I hate my life now,* she decided. *Before, everything was happy and good. Why did everything have to change?*

Molly Jean Harris, was born on August 12, 1946 to Walter and Fran Harris. Until then, the couple were the proud parents of four boys, ranging from eight to twelve. Fran, then forty one, had figured she was through having babies, and was stunned when her doctor told her she was pregnant.

"Fran, I have the results of your tests," the doctor noted over the phone.

Fran took a deep breath and acknowledged his remark. She was convinced it was something serious. Her father died two years before from cancer, and her mother had been suffering for sixteen years with Parkinson's Disease.

"Okay doctor, tell me what is going on." She spoke the words hesitantly, as she gripped Walter's hand on her end of the phone. Walter gently squeezed her hand when he saw her mouth drop open and a tear flow down her suddenly ashen cheek.

"What is it?" He tried not to sound too panicky.

"What did you say?" Fran managed to stammer to her physician. "Please speak slowly and clearly so I can be sure I understand you correctly."

Fran heard the words again. She had heard correctly the first time.

"You are going to have a baby. It is now two months along. Congratulations."

Quickly she handed the phone to Walt and ran from the room.

"Sweetheart, are you all right?" Walt found his wife of twenty-three years sitting on their porch, rocking and staring in disbelief.

"Quite a surprise, isn't it? I thought Bobby would be our last. Oh well, it would be nice if this one was a girl."

"How can you be so calm?" she asked. "I am forty- one years old and you're forty- two. We'll both be a year older when the child is born. Do you realize what this means? I don't know if I want to start with another baby."

"Darling, things will work out. You'll feel differently when the shock wears off. You're such a good mother and you love your sons. You have to give this child a chance. We'll manage."

Fran wore her strawberry blonde hair at shoulder length. It was laced with a few strands of gray which Walter told her made her look distinguished.

"Don't do that!" he protested when she told him she was going to have the gray rinsed out. "Those gray hairs look silver to me, and I think they make you look even more beautiful and distinguished."

"You'd tell me I looked beautiful if all my hair fell out and I developed warts," she laughed, looking at her man admiringly.

He always knew the right thing to say.

Fran loved her family and had always been glad she didn't have to work out of the home. After working as a waitress for three years while Walter finished school, she decided to go to college herself. He had received his degree in journalism and landed a job with the Boston Globe soon after graduation. He worked hard to help her go on with her studies, and she became a certified elementary school teacher. It took her five years to get her degree, and she was able to land a job at Hawthorne Elementary School where she had done her student teaching the year before. She taught fifth grade there for one year when she found out she was pregnant with her first child. The first thing she did when she learned the news was to turn in her resignation. Over the years, Walter had worked his way up the to the position of editor and financially they were doing very well.

Two years before their first child, the Harris' moved into their dream house. It was an old house built in 1714 and right on the historic trail in Salem. After getting it in shape and up to regulation, they had it registered with the national historic society. Proudly they nailed the plaque which read BUILT IN 1714 on the outside wall. They were proud of their house and couldn't wait to fill it with lots of children.

They had tried for eleven years to have children and began to think maybe they weren't able. Both she and Walt had been tested and told everything was fine. They had even begun to consider adoption. Then Fran missed her period and began to hope. When she missed it the next month, she went to see the doctor and received the good news.

105

"I'll get it," she yelled when the phone rang.

After listening for a few minutes, she hung up and returned with a sly look on her face.

"What is it?" he asked, "Did we win something?"

"Sort of," she said. " I'm pregnant."

What a difference between then and now, Fran thought. She realized she had been sitting in the same spot for at least a half hour now. Maybe Walter's right. I do have to give it a chance. I have always longed for a little girl. Maybe this will be her.

When Walt returned with Fran's drink, she looked up at him and smiled.

"Let's go tell the boys the good news," she grinned..

He breathed a sigh of relief as he reached out his hand to help her up. *How I love this woman,* he thought happily.

The following August, Walter arrived at work handing out cigars left and right.

"It's a beautiful baby girl," he beamed. "She was born at eleven last night, and weighed six pounds eight ounces."

The years had been good to Walt, and he was a young forty three. Holding his little girl, his face beamed with pride. Finally his family seemed complete.

Molly was a happy, rambunctious, carefree child, who loved to run and play and be with her brothers.

"She's too much of a tomboy," Fran would scowl as she watched Molly climbing trees like a pro. Fran knew she complained a lot, but she was extremely proud of her daughter.

Philip, the oldest, was thirteen when Molly was born and from the time she came home, he considered her to be his.

"Let me do it, mom," he'd say when she got ready to feed the baby. He was even willing to change her diapers when the other boys turned up their noses.

"Gross - how can you do that?" Mike, asked.

As Molly grew, Fran would often find Phil in her room telling her stories or teaching her games. A few times she found the door closed and became concerned.

"I think you should keep the door open," she mentioned to Phil one day.

"Mom, we were only having a tea party," he noted with impatience. "Jeez, she's my sister for Christ's sake, what do you think we do?"

"Watch how you talk to me," she reprimanded.

"Sorry, mom." He immediately calmed down.

"I just don't think it's proper somehow. I can't explain why but just humor me for now." she patted his cheek and walked away.

Phil rolled his eyes and retreated to his own room. For the rest of the time until he left for college, when he and Molly were together he left the door open, at least when he knew there were others around.

Molly was five when Philip went to college, and she cried uncontrollably when he left. She adored her oldest brother and feared he'd never return. Eventually, she began to adjust, and starting kindergarten helped divert her attention. When he called, she would tell him about school and he told her he hung all the drawings he had sent her on his wall.

That year when he came home for the holidays, Molly was ecstatic. After that, each time he left became a bit easier. Then after his sophomore year, Phil transferred to the state college in Salem and planned to live at home. He had been having trouble keeping up with his studies and thought he was just homesick. Molly drew a big sign that stated "WELCOME HOME, PHIL" and her mom helped her bake a cake.

"Hooray - he's here!" she shouted, running out to meet him. "Now everything will be like it was before."

But even she began to notice there was something different about him.

"What's wrong with Philip?" she asked her mom a few days after his return. "He's not like he was before."

"I don't know, sweetie; maybe he just needs time to adjust to being home again."

Molly hoped her mom was right. One day Phil appeared in her doorway.

"Let's play a game," he said with a broad smile. Molly jumped up with glee and pulled out her favorite game of Chutes and Ladders.

"Okay!" She could hardly conceal her excitement. "I'll even let you go first."

Phil quietly entered her room. "No, let me teach *you* a new game," he smiled slyly. He gently closed the door behind him.

After that, there were several occasions when Fran would come upstairs to find him alone with Molly in her room with the door closed. Fran knocked and entered one day, and Molly was sitting on her brother's lap. The two were rocking peacefully.

"What is going on?" she shouted, not meaning to. "Molly, are you sick?"

Molly shook her head no. " She's a little sad about something and I was trying to comfort her," responded Phil. Fran picked up the chagrin in his voice.

"I want this door to be left open from now on," she demanded. "Also, I don't think it is proper for you two to be alone together. Molly, if you are sad, you can talk to me."

"God, mother - don't you trust your own son?" Phil screamed as he stormed out of the room.

Phil remained very aloof after that, and Molly became more and more pensive. Fran noticed she would sometimes disappear for long periods of time, and come home smelling like pine needles.

"Where do you go so often?" she casually asked Molly one day when her daughter had been gone an exceptionally long time. "You look like you were in a fight."

Her clothes were wrinkled and dirty, and her hair was a mess.

"What do you care?" Molly glared at her. She had fallen asleep under her tree but was not going to tell her mother that.

Fran chalked the impertinence up to growing pains. She knew Molly had recently started her period, she would soon turn twelve, and she was about to start junior high school. So, with a gentle reminder to show some respect, she allowed Molly her space.

On her twelfth birthday Phil took Molly out for a special dinner and movie. When they got home, Fran was on the phone and Molly's brothers and dad were watching a wrestling match on TV.

"How was the movie?" Walter called to his daughter and son.

"Okay," said Molly. Walter looked up when he heard the sadness in her voice.

"She's okay," remarked Phil." It was a real tear jerker."

The two of them went upstairs together.

Phil had been living at home, trying to find a job, but not trying very hard. He had barely made it through college three years before and had a few odd jobs, but nothing steady. When he did get a job, it never seemed to last.

"It's just not my style," he'd complain. "The boss doesn't like me. I need something that pays better," were some of his many excuses.

His last job, which Walter had stuck his neck out to help Phil get, lasted two months when he came storming home.

"What the hell do they know anyway?" Phil slammed his things down. He had been fired that morning.

Fran and Walt often had heated discussions about his laziness.

"He is twenty-five years old. He needs to find his own place or pay board," yelled Walt. "He needs to show some responsibility and stick with a job. He'll never change if we continue to coddle him."

Finally Fran relented and agreed with her husband. Walter was planning to tell Phil the following morning.

Three weeks later Phil found a place with his friend Tony and moved out. Fran assumed this was why Molly was being so obnoxious, yet when she suggested Molly go visit Phil, she adamantly refused.

I'll never understand teenagers if I live to be a hundred, she thought. She vowed to speak to a friend who was on the same PTA committee. Rhonda had four girls and Fran wanted to be sure Molly's actions were typical. Some days, Molly seemed so withdrawn that it scared her.

Chapter Fourteen

"Cock - a - doodle - doo. Time to wake up and begin another day," the radio blasted up the stairs.

Fran played this same station every morning, thinking it was a creative way to wake her children. Molly hated it.

"Why can't she be like other parents?" Molly screamed silently as she pushed her blankets aside,. "It's so impersonal being awakened like this."

In reality, Molly would have hated anything Fran tried. She hated getting up and abhorred going to school. She had tried every excuse possible in the last year, but Mom never listened. Dad would just yell and tell her to grow up.

"Get your ass out of bed and get to school," he'd yell. "You're twelve years old now - it's time to grow up. You can fool your mother, but I know you're just faking. I won't take anymore. Now get moving."

She remembered arriving at school the day following her last illness and being called in to the counselor's office.

"Your dad called me earlier and told me you weren't really sick yesterday. He asked me to talk to you about your attendance. Is there anything I can help you with, Molly?"

Molly left the office feeling embarrassed and alone. *Isn't there anyone I can trust?* she thought. *Why can't people understand?*

After that, she trusted no one with her feelings. She put on a great show of being happy, but inside all she wanted to do was die.

Getting out of bed, her thoughts remained unchanged. *I wish I could get away from here. Why can't anyone see how miserable I am. Things have been this way for so long, and I did nothing to deserve it. Why is God punishing me?*

She dressed slowly and quietly out of habit. Her enthusiasm and optimistic outlook had vanished long ago. Everything she did lately, she did in a trance, by habit. Nothing was innovative or creative. She wasn't living, just surviving. "Hi, Molly. You look very nice," her mother greeted her as she walked into the kitchen.

Fran said the same words every morning. She no longer knew how to speak to her daughter. She could say the same thing two days in a row. One day Molly would smile and say thank you, and the next day Molly would curse at her and run from the room in tears. She did not know her daughter any more.

You say that all the time, Molly was thought angrily. *Why can't you see how sad I am and help me?*

Molly, Fran thought. She feared for her only girl child, *I know you're hurting. Please let me in. I want to help, but I can't reach you anymore.*

As usual, Walter said nothing verbally, but his scowl spoke volumes to Molly.

She just needs to stop her selfish attitude and become part of the family again, were the words spinning in his head. *What happened to my happy little girl?* His scowl was covering up the sadness and loss he really felt.

Bobby, the youngest of her four brothers, was already finishing up his breakfast and sharing his plans for the day. He was seventeen and now in his junior year in high school. He loved school and was involved in everything.

"Don't you think you're taking on too much?" Walt asked one day when Bob announced he joined the yearbook committee.

"Dad," he quickly responded, "I love being busy - you know that. These are the best years of my life; I want to take advantage of them."

Molly rolled her eyes. Bob played football in the fall and base-ball in the spring. He was assistant editor of the school paper, pres-ident of the National Honor Society, treasurer of the junior class, and was now working on the school yearbook.

What's wrong with me? she wondered again. So many times her parents would ask, *"Why can't you be more like Bobby, Brian and Mike?" I can't seem to do anything right. I'm such a loser. No won-der they hate me,* she thought.

Brian was two years older than Bob and a Freshman at Boston College. He was there on a scholarship for his football skills and doing extremely well. Mike, twenty-three, graduated from Salem State College, his dad's alma mater. He worked in Lynn as a high school math teacher and was studying for his Master's degree in the evenings.

Mom and Dad are so proud of them and hate me, she often told herself. *What am I going to do?*

She was a sixth-grader at North Salem Junior High School and hated it. The kids hated her, at least that was Molly's perception.

That afternoon Molly again walked home alone. "Why can't I make the kids like me?" she whined, "What did I do to them?"

The truth was that Molly was a loner and never attempted to socialize with her classmates. She never smiled and always chose a seat in the back of the room by herself. Kids had tried to be her friend, but she would just shrug and mumble that she was tired and needed to be alone. " I don't feel like going to the movie tonight." "Nah, I hate playing miniature golf." " I can't come over tonight - I need to watch my favorite TV program." She had an excuse for turning down every attempt her peers had made to include her. They finally gave up trying.

Teachers tended to ignore her, and she never volunteered an answer or joined in a class discussion.

"She is physically present but not really participating or mak-ing any effort," Miss Ash, her science teacher, informed her parents during open house. "She barely passes the tests, but I also base part of my students' grades on participation in discussions. Their input shows me they are thinking and using information, not just feeding it back to me on a test paper.

"If you don't mind me saying so, maybe what Molly needs is to talk to a psychologist or other professional. I believe she has some deeper problems," Miss White, the school counselor responded. Mr. and Mrs. Harris made it a point to stop and speak with her after hearing basically the same report from all her teachers. She was passing but just passing.

"I tend to think you're right," Fran confirmed what Miss White was saying. "I notice it at home also."

"That's nonsense!" Walt stood up in a rage. "She's fine. She's just lazy and feeling sorry for herself. Are you insinuating we're bad parents and don't know how to raise our own daughter? We're going home. Come on, Fran." He stormed out of the room. Fran apologized to the woman and followed her husband to the car.

Walter knew the words were true, but couldn't bring himself to face the problem. Something had happened to change his little girl and it scared him. He had always been able to fix things, but was helpless now. He didn't dare look back to see if his wife was approaching. He couldn't let her see the tears in his eyes.

"What are we going to do?" he prayed desperately. Discussing what they heard, they decided to wait and see if she would come out of her depression. "It's a phase," Walter said. "She'll come out of it in time. You wait and see." Fran nodded in agreement, wishing her heart would agree with her head.

Somehow, "Mopey Molly", as the kids called her, made it through seventh and eighth grade. She did every project alone because no one wanted to be her partner. Whenever partners were assigned for class activities, she endured the snickers and jeers of her classmates.

"You lucky kid," they'd chant sarcastically to the person assigned to be her partner. "Good luck with old pouty-puss. Don't let her touch you or you'll get cooties."

"Why don't we split the work now and each do our part on our own?" her co-worker would suggest.

114

"Sure," said Molly, holding back the tears. "That's fine with me."

Junior high was really a lonely time for Molly Harris. To make matters worse, things weren't much better at home.

"They only tease you because they like you," her mother would say when she tried to talk about her problems. "If you just ignore them, they'll stop."

"You're imagining things," her dad accused. "You're just making excuses for your bad attitude and dwindling grades. If you didn't just sit in front of the TV all the time and went out and tried to make friends, you wouldn't be so miserable."

So Molly's grades continued to slide, she continued to grow more sullen, and depressed, and her temper raged more frequently.

Then one day in October, while taking a test in Mr. Colbert's English class, Molly heard her name over the loud speaker.

"Will Molly Harris please report to the principal's office right away," was the announcement.

Mr. Colbert kindly informed her she could make up the rest of the test later and let her go.

Quickly, she picked up her books and hurried out of the room. She hated being singled out and felt everyone was watching her. In reality, they had all gone back to their work immediately following the announcement. No one saw her leave.

She was not prepared for what she heard when she arrived at Mr. Landerfield's office.

"Molly, your dad has had a heart attack and is in serious condition at Salem Hospital. Your mom is on her way to pick you up. Why don't you get your things from your locker then come back and wait for her? I'm really sorry," he said, putting his hand on her shoulder." Really sorry."

An hour later Molly and her mom arrived at Salem Hospital to the cardiac care unit. All of her brothers were there, as was Gina, Mike's wife and Tony, Phil's significant other. Phil had announced last June that he was a homosexual, causing more problems in the Harris household. His parents had disowned him immediately.

"We don't want 'queers' in this house," Walt sneered. "Take your things and get out. Don't ever come back, you hear?"

Fran looked away when Phil looked her way for some support. She said nothing. He shrugged, grabbed his jacket and left, never looking back.

Walter was hooked up to all kinds of machines and Molly nearly fainted when she saw him.

"We believe he'll pull through," she vaguely heard the doctor telling her mom." However, he's going to have to make drastic changes in his lifestyle."

Six weeks later, Walter arrived home with his list of "can's" and "can'ts". By far the "can'ts" outnumbered the "can's". The first on the list was: 'can no longer hold a full time job!'

The holidays weren't much fun that year. Walter just laid around, trying to get his strength back. Phil was not allowed in the house so went to Tony's for Christmas. Mike and Gina came for Christmas dinner and then hurried to her folks, who lived in Danbury, Connecticut which was a good three-hour ride.

Fran had the turkey at noon so they could get to Connecticut before dark. Even opening the presents wasn't much fun. Brian played the role of Santa since Walter was too tired. Bob was feeling sad and didn't really participate much. He had invited Annie, his girlfriend to dinner, and she had told him she couldn't come and that there was someone else in her life now.

After dinner, Fran made the announcement that she had been hired at Hawthorne Elementary School beginning in January. One of the fourth grade teachers was going on maternity leave and would not be back after the holidays, so Fran had a job at least until June.

"What the hell do you need a job for?" Walter hollered, obviously stunned at the announcement, "I have always supported this family and I'll continue to do that. There is no need for you to work."

"It's only for six months, Walt." Fran spoke calmly, but with determination. "You know you must take it easy and then go back to work only part time. My income will help out for now."

"No! I won't have it! Call and tell them you changed your mind."

"I can't - I signed the contract," she continued. "Let's enjoy dessert and discuss this later."

"I'm through." Walter threw down his napkin and left the room.

Some Christmas, Molly thought.

She could hear her parents arguing until quite late that night, and she cried herself to sleep.

On January 3rd, Fran dropped Molly at school and went on to meet her class for the first time. Walt spent the day home alone, feeling sorry for himself. When Molly arrived at two o'clock, he was sitting at the kitchen table with a drink in his hand, one of the "can'ts" on his list.

"Well, welcome home," his words slurred together. "Take a good look at this useless old man. Aren't you going to give your old man a kiss? Are you ashamed of me?"

Molly stood and stared at him, then ran to her room. A few minutes later, she heard him in the bathroom and then all was quiet. She tiptoed out to find him asleep on the couch, not knowing whether to feel sorry or angry.

He was unshaven, unkempt, and smelled like scotch. From that moment on, all sorrow and anger dissipated - all she could feel was shame for her father.

Fran arrived home at four and started supper. She woke Walt when it was time to eat. If she realized he had been drinking, she said nothing. Talk at the dinner table was strained and superficial. Mom said nothing about her new job and Dad didn't ask. Molly sat and stared.

I wish I were old enough to get out of here, she thought.

"Molly Jean Harris," the principal called as Molly stood to get her diploma. Finally she was leaving junior high and was determined that high school would be different.

Fran and Walter sat proudly watching their youngest child graduate from North Salem Junior High. She received no honors or awards, but she did pass and would be moving on. Secretly, they both hoped high school would be better for her. They knew she had had a rough time of it in school these past three years yet they didn't realize just how rough.

Things had calmed down at home since January. Walt had learned to accept Fran's working, and had taken early retirement from the paper. He was working mornings at Randall's Market, a small variety store down the street. He knew the owner well and could walk to work daily. He would arrive at seven and work until noon. He had to admit that his doctor was right - by the time he got home, he was exhausted. Walt still drank too much, but no one seemed to take notice - no one except Molly. She would come home to find him sprawled on the couch every afternoon. She would shake him awake so he could get cleaned up before Fran got home. It was becoming the normal routine at the Harris home.

January to June were torture for Molly at school. A few of the girls came and welcomed her back after vacation and asked how her father was doing.

"He's okay," she answered, grateful for their interest. "He's got to take it easy and that bothers him, but he's getting stronger every day."

She answered all their questions and thought maybe she finally might make new friends. Then she arrived in the cafeteria to hear the girls telling everyone her secrets and fears. The laughter and snickering were deafening, and Molly ran out of the room crying.

I should have known, she thought to herself. *I should know better than to trust people.*

She skipped her afternoon classes and took refuge under her tree. It seemed funny to be there again. She hadn't visited her "secret place" since she started junior high. She sat and cried until two, then went in the house. It seemed like all she did lately was cry.

Monday, March 12, was the date that would be etched in her mind forever. It was the day her nightmare began.

She was writing her essay for Mr. Colbert and cringing. Hal, the boy behind her, was scribbling on her new white blouse - at least that's what it felt like. She wanted to turn around and pound him, but could only pretend to ignore him. She could hear the kids around her giggling as she got up to leave when class ended.

"Hal, come here," she heard Mr. Colbert call.

When she got home, Molly threw her new blouse in the trash, as tears rolled down her cheeks. She could tell no one. That night she decided to run away.

"I can't go to school today," she whined. "I have a splitting headache and ache all over."

Fran allowed her to stay home and told her to stay in bed.

"She's not really sick," she told Walter, " but something is wrong. I figured maybe she needed the day off."

When her parents left for work, Molly quickly got dressed and grabbed her savings from her secret hiding place. Downstairs, she opened Mom's drawer and stole fifty dollars from the food money. Molly headed for the train station. She had decided to go to Mike and Gina's house. Gina was a nurse and worked three evenings a week, so she would be home. They lived in Rowley, a small town north of Salem. She would have to take a train to Ipswich, and then call Gina to pick her up or take a taxi. Having looked at the train schedule the night before, Molly knew there was a train going to Ipswich at ten thirty.

"Gina, this is Molly. I'm at the Ipswich train station. Can you pick me up?"

"Molly, what are you doing there? Aren't you supposed to be in school?"

"I ran away," Molly confided in her sister- in -law, "Please come - it's getting cold."

"I'll be there in about twenty minutes. Why don't you go in Woolworth's down the street and I'll meet you there."

About half hour later, Molly spotted Gina's red Camaro and hopped in. Neither one of them spoke on the ride back to Rowley.

Gina fixed Molly a chicken sandwich and some tomato soup.

"Eat this," Gina stated, "then we'll talk."

Gina listened to Molly without interruption. For the first time in a long time, Molly felt like she had an ally. She could tell Gina really did believe her.

"You poor kid," she managed to say. "Why don't you stay and relax until Michael arrives, and we'll decide what to do then. Do you want to lie down or just watch TV?"

"TV, I guess." Molly felt drained after sharing her deepest secrets. "Thanks for listening."

"I can appreciate your problems, but running away is not going to help," Mike tried to tell her later that afternoon. "Mom and dad are probably frantic wondering where you are. I think you should at least call and tell them."

Molly could only sit in stunned silence, tears rolling down her face. When will someone understand how I feel, and help me? she wondered. She couldn't see that they were trying to help the best way they knew how. Mike looked at his wife helplessly. He loved his kid sister, but couldn't allow her to avoid things. He had spoken to his parents earlier from work, and they had conceived a plan.

"Dad, this is Mike. Gina just called me. Molly is at our house. She informed Gina she was running away. I thought I should let you know. She has no idea I'm calling you. Dad, what are we going to do? The kid needs help."

"Mike, thank God you called. I arrived home about forty-five minutes ago, and found Molly's note. I was frantic and feeling helpless. Her note says:

'I am running away. I hate my life here.
If you try to find me and bring me home, I'll kill myself.'

"I did call Miss White at the school. She suggested a man in Salem who might be able to help, a doctor named Liston. If you can convince her to call us, I'll arrange to bring her immediately to his office. Don't tell her or she'll never agree to call home."

"I'll do that." Mike hung up and stared straight ahead.

"Molly, I hope we're doing the right thing. Please know we have only your best interests at heart." He reluctantly went back to his class.

"Fine," she snorted. "I'll call. Thanks for your understanding and support," she added sarcastically as she walked from the room. It was three thirty.

Two hours later, her parents arrived to bring her home, or so she thought.

"Where are we going?" Molly questioned when they suddenly turned right instead of left. "Where are you taking me?" she yelled when neither responded to her first question. "What are you doing?" She began to panic.

Then she saw the sign which read SALEM HOSPITAL, and started to sob uncontrollably.

"Why are we stopping here?" she stammered, hardly able to get the words out.

"Darling." Her mom spoke gently. "We thought you needed some help and called Dr. Liston. He's a very nice man and wants to talk with you. Won't you at least see him this once?"

"What - is he a 'shrink?" Molly's voice was soft and quivering.

"He's a child psychologist, yes," Walt roared," "and you will see him *now*."

Afraid of what would happen if she refused, she got out of the car and walked between her parents to meet this great Dr. Liston.

Dr. Steven Liston, Licensed Psychologist, read the words on the office door. There were no other people in the waiting room when the Harrises entered. Everything looked sterile and new.

"May I help you?" asked the petite black woman behind the glass partition.

"We have an appointment to see the doctor," Fran explained. "The patient's name is Molly Harris."

Molly was devastated when she heard her mother's words. She couldn't believe they had this all arranged without even talking to her about it. She was angry with them, but more importantly, she was scared to death.

"Hi. You must be Molly," Dr. Liston put out his hand when Lakeisha, the receptionist, escorted them to his office.

"I spoke to your parents on the phone earlier today, and they sounded so concerned that I stayed late just to see you. How can I help you, Molly?"

She just sat there and stared straight ahead. He was about thirty-five, had thinning black hair with graying sideburns. He was maybe forty pounds overweight for his short stature. He seemed fake to Molly, and his smile seemed pasted on.

"Molly." He gently tried to bring her back. She was so scared she could not speak. Tears flowed down her cheeks as her heart seemed to be breaking. Her whole world was falling apart, and she was a victim of some fiendish plot. She knew she should defend herself, but no words would come. Her feelings of betrayal were only surpassed by her feeling of sheer panic.

Lakeisha came in and brought Molly to an inner waiting room, where she gave her a glass of water and tried to calm her down.

"I think we should admit her," Dr. Liston confided to her parents. "Let's give it a week and see how she is after that. What do you think?"

"It's up to you," Fran noted. "You're the expert. We just want her to get help."

She had looked so thin and pale when his receptionist brought her from the room. Her heart ached when she watched Molly's shoulders shake with fear.

Walter looked at the young man and nodded.

"Do what you think is necessary, Doc." His slumped shoulders and empty eyes showed how much he wanted to have his happy little Molly back.

"I know you both probably feel that she hates you and will never forgive you. Trust me - I've seen this before, and it is the only way to avoid her possibly doing harm to herself. I believe I can help her. Why don't you go home, get some rest, and I'll get Molly settled in next door. I'll call you in the morning and let you know about visiting hours, and you can bring her things then. It'll be better for her, if you leave quietly without seeing her again. Please believe me that Molly is not beyond help, and I am confident I can reach her."

Silently, the couple walked to the car hand in hand. Neither saw the other's pained face as they left their little girl behind.

Each morning from ten to eleven, Molly went to see "Steve". Every evening, she would turn her back when her parents came to visit her. She said nothing and ate little. She was in a semi-private room, but at the moment the other bed was unoccupied. The TV was constantly on, but Molly's stare was not even aware of it. It was as if her body was there but her spirit had left completely.

Even Dr. Liston was beginning to become concerned. He had been sure he could reach her, but their sessions were just one hour of silence.

"Molly, how can I help you? Can you tell me what's bothering you? Trust me - I'll tell no one, and I'm trained to help you." Her empty eyes stared straight ahead and she said nothing. "You have pretty eyes," he'd utter as he noticed the fear in them. "I bet you have a lot of things inside you. Can't you just try me? I promise I'll understand." Nothing.

This scenario was the same each morning, and the nurses informed him it was the same thing with them.

"It's as if she's in another world, and her body just responds out of habit. She goes through the motions, but isn't really present," the head nurse told him.

"Molly, it's us. We brought you a present. One of your classmates brought it by. She said the kids wanted to let you know they were thinking of you, and gave her the job of buying the gift. Can you at least accept it?" After a few minutes, Fran pleaded again. "Please Molly, let them care."

Slowly, Molly turned over and took the small package.

"Nice time to show concern." Her words were biting. "What is it? Probably it's some gag or something. They don't care about me!"

Suddenly, Molly threw the package and its contents against the wall and went into a rage.

"I hope and hope, again and again, and all I do is get hurt! No one gives a damn about me! Why do I keep believing things will be different? What the hell does everyone think - that I'm stupid or something? I have feelings, too. I'm not crazy or insane. I only want someone to care and love me. Is that so much to ask for? That's all I've ever wanted and all I get is shit! Tell them to take their god-dam gift and shove it. Just get out and leave me alone!"

Fran and Walt stood rooted. They couldn't believe the fury they saw. It was as if a time bomb that had been building in Molly had exploded. No one seemed to be able to stop her tirade.

The nurse had run for Dr. Liston, who arrived in time for the last few words. He ordered some medication for Molly, and escorted her parents out of the room when the nurses arrived with the syringe. He reached down and picked up the ring which had fallen from the package on the way out.

That night, Molly slept quietly. At home, Walter sat downstairs, drank his scotch and stared at the blank TV screen and Fran tossed around in the bed, wondering where they had gone wrong. What had happened that would cause a simple ring to set off such an explosion? She felt like such a failure as a mother.

Tentatively Molly opened the small package her mother had brought her. To her surprise it was a very pretty, monogrammed ring. Molly held it for a minute, deep in thought.

"Maybe they really do care," she mumbled, forgetting she wasn't alone. "Maybe they *are* trying to be friendly. Maybe I should give them a chance."

Looking again at the ring, she began to hope that maybe things were changing. She went to try on the ring and something inside of her snapped. She couldn't keep her feelings inside any longer. Her rage and fury let loose in front of everybody, and for once she didn't care. How could they be so thoughtless? The next thing she knew, the nurses were trying to calm her, and the doctor was taking her parents out of the room. She couldn't even yell for them she was sobbing so much. She felt a prick in her arm, and suddenly felt sleepy and weak. The nurses had given her a sedative. In a matter of minutes she was fast asleep.

"It was a 'W', she mumbled to Dr. Liston the next morning. "The initial was a 'W'".

He had asked her gently if she remembered the previous night. Now he had a look of confusion on his face when she looked at him. "What do you mean, Molly?" he coaxed.

"The monogram on the ring was "W" and my name begins with an M. Can't you see?" she quivered, fighting tears." They just don't care - no one does."

"It could have been a mistake," he responded kindly. " Maybe the girl who chose it thought it was an M. Mistakes happen, Molly."

"No, if they cared they'd get it right. They can't even get my name right. What did I ever do?" She held her face in her hands and sobbed.

Steve Liston walked from behind his desk and put his hand on her shoulder. "It's okay Molly - let it all out."

A week later, Steve informed Molly that he felt she was ready to go home. She had come a long way that week, and he was sure she'd be okay.

"Use the little tools I suggested, and you'll do okay," he smiled at her. "You're one tough cookie, and you can make your world better. Just take each day as it comes, and if you need to talk I'll be here. Your folks care, and you can talk to them."

"I will doctor - thank you." She shook his hand and went out to the car while her parents talked to her doctor.

She had talked to him every day, but only said what he wanted to hear. She told him surface stuff, normal teenage problems, and convinced him she was better. She had long ago become a great actor, and knew if she was to get out of there she'd have to be believable. She was cooperative, pleasant, and polite. She agreed to everything he had asked of her, and told him her "problems". Little did he know, she was just bullshitting him. At that very moment, she vowed to herself things would be different.

March 28, two weeks after her ordeal began, Molly returned to school, and endured the last two and one half months. She spoke when she had to, answered questions when asked, and ignored the jeers of others. She had circled graduation on her calendar and lived for that day.

Finally, the day she longed for arrived, and she was slowly walking up the steps to get her coveted diploma. She looked straight ahead and saw no one. All she could think of was getting out of there for good.

They'll all pay when I get to high school, she thought, *they'll be sorry they tangled with Molly Jean Harris.*

"Molly, Molly." She heard her name and finally realized where she was. Opening her eyes, she noted Dr. Strong smiling at her from across the room. Slowly Molly sat up. She felt like a wrung-out dishrag.

"How do you feel, Mol?" It was Linda speaking from a chair beside the couch.

"I'm really tired. I feel like I fought a war," she responded candidly. Rubbing her eyes, she realized she had been crying a great deal.

"You should feel that way," Dr. Strong answered. "You worked very hard this evening. You remembered a lot. Molly," he touched her hand, "You did very well."

Smiling, he bid them adieu and left the two women alone.

"I'm very proud of you, Molly," Linda smiled at her. "Why don't you get some sleep, and we'll continue the same time tomorrow evening."

That night Molly slept better than she ever had before.

Chapter Fifteen

"Okay, Molly, let's begin." Dr. Strong's soothing voice helped her to relax even more. "Go back to the secret place where you started yesterday. Tell us what you remember, but tonight we may ask you some questions."

Suddenly Molly was back in her secret place. Yet she didn't remember being quite as sad as the previous night.

High school was rough on Molly. She had dreamed all summer that she would enter Salem High and everything would be different. It didn't turn out that way.

"Molly, time to get up. Molly!" Mom was calling her from the hallway.

Soon she was dressed in a cheery, colorful, outfit bought new that summer, and was proud of the way she looked. This new tenth grader even tried donning some make-up. Feeling truly pleased with her looks, she bounced downstairs to breakfast, smiling and raring to go.

"What's that you got on your face?" her dad mocked. "My God - it's make-up. You've got too much on. Don't you even know how to put make-up on? What kind of girl are you if you can't 'paint' your face right? And don't you think that dress is too bright? Whoever picked it out for you has awful taste. You look like a clown, for crying out loud."

"What do you care, anyway!" she yelled back at him.

Molly left the room in tears. Slamming the bathroom door, she scrubbed and scrubbed her face until it was raw. Then she ran to her room and dumped all her new cosmetics into the trash.

How can he be so mean? she thought. *Why does everyone always have to criticize? Can't they help instead? People always manage to tell you what you do wrong, but never give advice on how to improve. Can't dad at least give me credit for trying to improve?*

"She looked very nice," Fran said to her husband. "You know she's nervous about school. Couldn't you find something good to say?"

"Oh, teenage girls! I'll never understand. I always say the wrong thing. From now on I'll just shut up!" he responded sarcastically. Taking his coffee with him he left for work.

Fran knocked quietly on her daughter's door. She knew things that Mol didn't. Her husband was under a lot of stress at work. Phil was just diagnosed to be HIV positive but didn't want anyone else to know, and Walt grew up with six brothers and felt very uncomfortable trying to talk to a teenage girl. She knew how much Walt loved his daughter. The problem was he didn't know how to show the love and pride he felt. He could tell everyone but Molly. However, Fran, receiving no response to her knock, opened the door and found the room empty.

Molly had left quietly out the front door. Her heart was no longer into school. She just wanted to curl up and die.

The ride to school seemed endless as Molly stared out the window of the bus thinking, *I try so hard to get Dad to like me. Why can't he? What's wrong with me?*

Just as expected, Molly's first day was a disaster all around. Her locker wouldn't open no matter how hard she tried. It turned out she had been given the wrong combination. Because of this she was late for her first class and everyone stared when she walked in. What made it worse was that her teacher noted her tardiness loudly.

"I will not tolerate tardiness in my class. From now on you will get here on time, understood?"

Nodding, Molly Harris walked to the one remaining seat and shrunk down into the chair. She was totally mortified. The rest of the day went even worse.

For Molly, her three years of high school was no better than junior high. Her dream of being accepted by her peers never became a reality. She buried herself in her studies and was a good student. Math turned out to be her strength and she excelled in those classes. She never did well in classes where participation was considered a part the grade. She understood the material and wrote excellent essays but she never offered an opinion or theory. Many times she had ideas and tried to volunteer but her hand would not go up. It was torture when one of her classmates offered the same thought as hers and the teacher would exclaim how accurate the idea was. For Molly, she had learned that it was best to just be agreeable. Risk only brought laughter and hurt.

After graduation, Molly took her gift money and all she had saved over the years and moved to New York. Riding the train to the end of the line, she ended up in Buffalo, got a room in the YWCA and started job hunting. Her third attempt of the day was a cute little shop called Patty's Pleasantries.

The ad in the paper asked for a receptionist, no experience necessary.

When Molly arrived at the lovely little shop, she was surprised to see the owner sitting there giving directions over the phone. The woman, Pat, motioned to her to take a seat and after a few moments, hung up the phone. Molly smiled as Pat related the mishaps which led up to her assuming the duties of receptionist. Molly's smile caused Pat's tone to change as she realized this woman had not come to hear her woes. She offered her hand to Molly, asking what she could do for her.

Molly liked Pat from that moment and was very much at ease with her. The feeling was mutual with Pat and Molly left the building an hour later with plans to return after lunch and a change of clothing. She had gotten the job.

Her new boss had suggested that Molly go have lunch and change into something a little more casual, then come back to begin work at one o'clock. In the meantime, she continued to hold down the fort. Molly walked back to the "Y" with a new-found bounce in her step.

Linda had been listening intently to Molly's words and feeling her pain. Noting that her patient was in a more positive place, she felt it was a good stopping point.

"You've done a great job, Mol," Linda said, as she gently touched Molly's shoulder. "Come back to us."

When her patient opened her eyes, Linda turned and smiled at Dr. Strong. The psychologist noticed those deep brown eyes had lost some of the pain and anger which they had held since she began working with Molly. She had known for a while now that there was much more behind the sadness than just her problems with Jake. However, the choice to delve further had to be up to her patient.

Never, never, push the patient to remember something. You'll know when the patient is ready! ran through Linda's mind. One of her professors, later her advisor when she did her clinical training, repeated this line again and again. In fact, it got to be a joke. When he started the total class would chant the sentences with him. He'd just laugh and say,"You'll see someday. Trust me."

Well, she saw what he meant, and thanked him in her heart.

For the rest of the week, Molly talked and remembered a great deal and was able to let go of a lot. Linda was a great help, as was Dr. Strong. Both were gentle, supportive, and helped Molly to feel at ease. The last day was the hardest for all of them. Yet it proved to be the true turning point for Molly Stelson.

"Ready, Molly?" Dr. Strong queried as the patient stretched out on the couch.

"Yes," she replied. "I'll meet you in my favorite space." They all laughed quietly at her remark, and Linda couldn't help but burst with pride at how far Molly had come in the past four days. She allowed Dr. Strong to continue, knowing tonight would be the toughest thing Molly would ever have to face. He was about to ask her about Phil.

Tears streamed down her face as if a cloud had burst behind her eyeballs. Molly's body stiffened, then went limp while she sobbed. Patiently they waited.

"Take your time, darling." Linda's voice was gentle. She knew her patient well enough to know that these tears were helping her to face the pain. Finally, her muffled words began.

Molly remembered the time she was four and Phil came into her room for a tea party. The two of them sat for a little while, then, suddenly he got up and closed the door. Molly got very scared and wanted to cry. Sitting back down he told her he loved me very much, and she was very special. He moved closer to her and began to stroke my hair. Then he was blowing on my neck and hugging me.

All of a sudden he stopped. There was a knock at the door, and Mommy came in and said she should keep the door open. Molly's voice was becoming that of a four year old. It was filled with terror.

"Another time Phil came to read me a bedtime story. We were sitting in the rocking chair and he was reading *Winnie the Pooh*. Back then I loved Pooh bear. Then he stopped reading. He put his hand down in my panties and started touching me. He rubbed my genitals and bottom. Then he put his finger in my rectum and my vagina. I didn't know the adult words, but I knew it hurt, and somehow it was wrong. I trembled but couldn't move. He kept whispering to me that I was special and what he was doing was special, between him and me. He said if I told Mommy and Daddy, they'd get mad and punish me. They'd stop loving me. I believed him.

He stopped suddenly when the door opened and Mom came in. She seemed to sense something was wrong. She told Phil, again, to leave the door open. He got mad, yelled at her and left my room.

"After that he would come in often. Usually in the night, he would come and lay beside me.

"'You are my special baby. I love you in a way I don't love anyone else. In the whole family, you are my favorite,' he would whisper in my ear as he fondled me.

"Sometimes, if he was baby-sitting during the day, he'd do it then. I hated it and I hated him. Other times it felt good, and I'd get afraid and ashamed."

Molly hesitated for a while sniffing, holding back tears. Linda, handing her a tissue, exclaimed, "Mol, I know this is hard for you but you are doing so well. Can you go on?"

"I cried when he went to college. I hated what he did, but I loved him a lot. He was always giving me things such as toys and dolls. He'd take me to the park and the pool. He would make me laugh. I think I loved and hated him at the same time.

"After two years he came home again. He changed colleges. He was different then. He didn't laugh as much, slept a lot during the day, and stayed out late at night. Somehow by then I had forgotten what he had done before. At least I thought I had.

"Then, one day I had just finished cleaning my room when he came in. He asked to play a game and I pulled out Chutes and Ladders. I was really too old, but it was 'our' game and I thought it would be fun. I hadn't played it since he left two years before.

"He shook his head and wanted to teach me a new game. He sat on my bed and beckoned me to come over. I cringed and began to shake. Suddenly I remembered.

"He told me we were alone in the house. He was in charge. If I didn't do what he said, he'd spank me. Then he began to take off my clothes. He was kissing me all over and even kissed my private parts. I wanted to push him away but I couldn't. It's like I was frozen stiff. I tried to think about other things till he finished. He kissed, touched, and fondled a long time; then he made me kiss his penis. I almost threw up, but made myself stop."

Molly screamed. "No, stop, it hurts. He's hurting me! Make him stop!"

"What, Molly?" Linda's voice was soothing and gentle. "What is he doing?"

132

"He's pushing his, his thing up inside me. God, he's hurting me!"

"When he left, I slowly got up. I went in to use the bathroom and saw blood. I sat on the toilet and cried. Then I went and got dressed. I must have fallen asleep, because Mom was waking me for supper. I couldn't eat and picked at my food. I could hear Phil saying, 'She was very good. No problem.'

"He would come into my room a lot after that. I was so scared every night going to bed that Mom was getting worried. She caught us a few more times alone in my room and one time she got real mad. I almost told her, but nothing came out of my mouth.

"When I was twelve, Phil moved out and I was thrilled. I hoped I would never see him again. I decided to try and tell my dad.

" 'Daddy.' I approached him sitting on the porch swing, relaxing. He liked to do that after dinner, sometimes. Since his heart attack, he would tire much more easily.

" 'Hi, sweetheart, come sit with me. It's such a nice night.'

" 'Dad, ever since I was little and mom used to give me baths, she's told me that it's not right for anyone to touch another person's private parts. Last year in health, Miss Troubalos, told us the same thing.'

"He stared at me not knowing where this was leading, but wanting to listen. 'That's right, doll,' he answered. 'Why?'

" 'Dad, before Phil left, he was touching me there. He told me he loved me in a special way... ' I held my breath and just blurted it all out, and didn't breathe until I finished. Relieved that it was out I waited for "MY" dad to go to Phil's and do something.

"Do you know what he did ? He stood up, opened his palm and slapped me hard, right across the face.

" 'Don't you ever speak like that about one of your brothers again. You are a liar and a slut. If it happened, which I doubt, you must have done something to attract him. I never want to hear of this again! Do you understand?' He slammed the door so hard, I thought it was broken.

"I ran to my tree, which I had discovered a few months before and sobbed and sobbed.

" 'Phillip was right! He was right! It *was* my fault! I am a bad person and deserve to be hated! I am no good! Now who will love me?"

"You are not a bad person, Molly. He was the bad one, not you. Darling, you were little. You had no control. Your father was wrong, and your brother was definitely wrong, but you have nothing to be ashamed of. Molly, Molly..."

Opening her eyes, Molly realized where she was. Dr. Strong gave her the "thumbs up" and quietly left. With her head on Linda's shoulder, Molly sobbed as if her heart would break.

After about half an hour, she felt drained, like a wrung-out dish cloth. Yet, at the same time, there was a lightness in her which she had never felt before. Molly was going to be okay.

Chapter Sixteen

It was a beautiful, sunny morning with only a few white clouds in the sky. Molly drove with her windows down breathing in the fresh, spring air. She was feeling freer and happier than she had felt in a long, long time.

The previous ten days had been hell for her but she had survived them. The excess baggage of pain, guilt, resentment and anger were gone now. Molly's past was truly behind her.

"You were suppressing all those feelings of disappointment and betrayal for a long time," Linda told her. "That is why the events of the recent past were so hard for you to endure. You didn't have the strength to fight those hurts, plus the ghosts of the past. The depression and rage won out."

"But not any more." Molly grinned an elated grin.

She had stayed on three extra days to recuperate from the grueling sessions with Dr. Strong. They finished on Saturday and she slept most of Sunday and until noon on Monday. Molly slept as if she had never slept before. Monday afternoon she met again with Linda, who helped her see how the pains of the past were hurting her in the present. Her beloved shrink gave her some practical ways to help herself when the past events tried to haunt her again.

"You can't deny these things happened, Molly," Linda explained. " But you can and must accept that it is part of who you are. Let me give you some tools which you can use when the memories creep up on you again."

Now Molly was heading home with these ideas planted deeply in her head, ready to begin her new life. She still planned to see

Linda once a month for support, but no longer needed to stay at the clinic.

"If you feel you really want to come for a few days," Linda added, "know that our doors are always open to you. However, I believe you can help yourself now as well as we can."

Yes, Molly thought, *I can and I will.* She pulled up to Pat and Sophie's condo with a determination to make a better life for herself and her little girl.

"Maggie is doing fine," Sophie assured her when she had called Saturday evening saying she needed a few more days. "She stayed a couple of nights at Rose's house, and her dad is taking her tonight to stay with him. He'll be picking her up shortly, and said he'd have her back by five tomorrow afternoon. Do you want me to tell him he can keep her a day longer?"

"No," Molly responded. " Just leave it the way it is. I'd rather she keep her routine with you on school days. Do you think she'll talk to me?"

Maggie came to the phone to Molly's delight. "Hi, baby. How are things going? I love you and will be home very soon."

"I'm okay," her daughter informed her. "I stayed at Rose's Tuesday and Wednesday night so we could finish our project for social studies. Pat and Sophie have been good to me. I miss you and wish you'd hurry home. Dad's here - I have to go. Mom.." she hesitated, then in a small voice continued, "I love you, too."

Neither Sophie nor Maggie mentioned to Jake that Molly was on the line. Pat got the details regarding her arrival home while Sophie waved goodbye to Mags.

When Sophie dropped Maggie at school Wednesday morning she immediately went to the Stelson home to make sure things were in order and to drop off Maggie's things. Molly planned to arrive home around 1:00 PM and would pick her little girl up from school. The housekeeper laughed when Molly kept talking about her "little girl". Maggie was almost ten now and sprouting up rapidly. She was nearly five feet tall, if not already there. She was going to be a very pretty girl.

There is something about Maggie that is very sad, Sophie noted to herself as she hung up Maggie's clothes. *The poor kid has had such a hard life so far.*

Finding the game her father had bought Mags caused Sophie to sit on the bed and ponder.

Jake dropped Maggie off at approximately 4:45 PM last Sunday, explaining that they had had a long, tiring day at the carnival in Buffalo. "We had a wonderful time, didn't we, princess?" He gave his daughter a big hug and kiss. Mags let him, but didn't hug him back or answer his question. When he drove off she simply said, "I'm tired. I think I'll go to my room," and strolled off. The two women just looked at each other in awe.

"I wonder what *that's* about?" Pat questioned. Sophie just shrugged an "I don't know".

"Hi!" The cheerful voice in the doorway startled Sophie, and coming out of her reverie, she jumped up to greet Mrs. Stelson.

"I was just finishing up in here and started thinking." She went over to her boss. "Molly, you look wonderful. How are you feeling? There's a sparkle about you that I've never seen before." Sophie wrapped her arms around her employer and hugged her.

After the two women visited for a while, Sophie left to give Molly some time to be home, before she had to pick up her daughter.

Molly let Sophie out and proceeded to take herself on a tour of her home. She saw everything with brand new eyes. It was as if she had been blind and suddenly given her sight back. Even the spots on the carpet were beautiful to her. After her tour, the woman went to her bedroom, opened the window to air it, grabbed all her pills and bottles and dumped them in the trash. She moved like a tornado and had the room completely cleaned before going to get Maggie at school. There was no trace of the other Molly left at all.

"Hey, Mag - there's your mom." Rose nudged her friend. Maggie was discussing a very important problem with Diane. She had relaxed this week and, because of Rose, was becoming more outgoing. Her circle of friends was growing.

Maggie groaned and turned around. At first she didn't recognize the woman standing there. Only when Molly smiled and waved did the girl know her mom. Mags walked over slowly, not knowing what to expect. Sophie had said Molly was better, but Maggie had learned not to trust appearances. She dared not hope things would be different.

Reaching her mom, Maggie looked up and half- smiled. "Hi," was all she could say.

"Hi, sweetie. Ready to go home?" When Molly spoke she hoped her voice didn't betray the fear she felt. All the way to school she continued to tell herself, *This is crazy to be afraid of your own daughter!* However, she couldn't help it. Molly accepted the role she had played in making Maggie's early life miserable, and she so wanted things to be different. "How was your day?" she asked while fastening her seat belt. "Okay," replied Maggie. They rode home in silence.

"Look, Mom - I need to put my things away and do my homework," Maggie said more curtly than she wished when Molly asked her to come into the kitchen for milk and cookies.

Molly just nodded and let her go. Then, she thought twice about her decision, and went after the girl.

"Maggie!" she called. The dark-haired, tall, lovely girl whom Molly knew as her baby, was half way up the stairs when she turned to look at her mother below.

Mol took a deep breath and continued. "Darling, I realize this must be awkward and confusing for you. It is for me, too. Please let your school work wait and join me. We need to talk and I don't think we can put it off. Sophie left some of her luscious cookies out. You can waste a half hour before starting you homework."

"All right." Maggie followed her mother into the kitchen. Her lack of enthusiasm and her determination not to talk were obvious.

"Maggie, I know I haven't been the best mother to you over the years, but I'm better now. I promise things are going to be different," Molly began as Maggie picked up a cookie. She would not even look at her mother.

Over an hour later, they were still there, and Molly had even managed to get Mags to laugh once or twice. Then in a moment of lapsed conversation Maggie asked, "Mom. What about dad?"

"I don't know, sweetheart," Mol answered honestly. "I just don't know if he can believe I've changed. He may still leave. I hope not, but he may need time to sort things out. I haven't been too nice to him either. Let's wait and see, shall we., baby?" Molly put her hand on her daughter's. "Whatever he does, try not to judge him too harshly. Promise?" Maggie nodded.

Jake came in very late to get the remainder of his things. He had been coming in a lot while she was away, picking up belongings and reminiscing about the happy times they had spent together. He was suddenly startled to hear Molly's voice. "H-h-h-hi," he stuttered. "W-w-w-what's up?" He was obviously caught off guard.

"Aren't you going to say anything?" Molly thought she was ready for this moment, but Jake's discomfort made her ill at ease. "I just got home from Rochester and I am much better."

"Oh, yeah, " he said quickly. "You look good." He stopped and stared at the woman before him. For a minute he remembered the young girl he had married and the fun times they used to have.

However the thoughts vanished rapidly, with the thought of Juli waiting in the car. He grabbed the last of his possessions and headed for the door.

"Molly, I'm glad you're better, really I am. But I'm not in love with you anymore. I want to be with Juli. We have made plans and I'm committed." It was as if he were trying to convince himself, more than his wife. "Besides, I think a time of separation will be good for both of us. Dad gave me a transfer to our offices in Detroit, and Juli is coming as my secretary. I'll get in touch with you after a few months and we can talk. Mol, I just need to figure things out. Please understand."

"What about Maggie? What do I tell our daughter? Will you see her at all?" Molly spoke with more courage than she felt.

"I don't know. Tell her I'll be in touch. I'm sorry, Mol." He turned and ran down the stairs. He decided to purchase what he needed rather than pack his things. He just had to get away as fast as he could.

Juliann noticed his empty hands and guessed what must have happened. She put her hand gently on his leg as he pulled the car away from the house. Her family was not too thrilled with her decision either. Detroit would be good for both of them.

They rode in silence for quite a while, then made small talk. Neither one talked about what they were leaving behind or future plans. They arrived in Michigan at six-thirty the following morning.

Chapter Seventeen

Molly couldn't believe she was preparing a "bash" as her daughter called it, for Maggie's sixteenth birthday. The party was to take place in ten days and she had been watching Rose and Maggie plan for weeks now. They agonized over the guest list and narrowed it down to a mere thirty kids. The dynamic duo shopped endlessly, searching for the most exquisite decorations. They even called their plans off three times over a squabble. Then, all of a sudden, the friends had reconciled their differences and had their heads together once more.

"It's your daughter's birthday," Denise Arlton informed Molly over the phone one day. "Yet I think my Rose is more excited than she is."

"Oh, is it on again?" Molly laughed. "Last I heard it was off because Maggie wanted to put pineapple in the punch and Rose thought the idea was too corny."

The two women laughed over the escapades of their daughters. However, when Molly had time to step back from the chaos she couldn't help thinking how great it was to see Maggie so happy and normal.

After Jake left six years before, Maggie seemed so distant and forlorn most of the time. Sometimes she'd smile, even laugh, but there always seemed to be a sadness in her eyes. At the same time, Maggie questioned almost everything her mother did.

"Where are you going?" "When will you be back?" "Why are you doing that?" and so on.

One day Maggie discovered her pills in the bathroom and screamed, "What are these? You told me you weren't taking a bunch of pills anymore. Why did you lie?" and ran from the room.

Molly heard the fear in Maggie's voice and cringed. "Sweetie, these pills really will make me well. They're called Zoloft and I'm to take one each morning. This is not like before. I won't take more than what's prescribed. Linda suggested I take them and she is the person who made me well. Maggie, believe me - I won't ever go back the way I was. I won't let myself. Please, darling - trust me."

It was to be a long time before Maggie truly trusted her mom. However, slowly the questions and comments dissipated and the tension between mother and daughter diminished.

Jake had called six months after he left and asked Molly for a divorce, informing her that his lawyer would be sending her the papers. All she had to do was sign them. When they arrived Mol took them to a lawyer Pat recommended. When she was satisfied they were all in order, she signed them. Neither she nor Maggie had heard from him since. Molly did see in the paper an announcement of the marriage between James Stelson III and Juliann Quarles.

"I wish you the best, Jake," she whispered silently, tears running down her face. Somewhere deep down inside, she had hoped he'd come back. Molly Harris Stelson still loved the man.

Two weeks after her return from Rochester, Pat approached Molly asking her if she wanted her old job back. Molly was thrilled with the idea. She dragged Maggie shopping with her, hoping to find an appropriate outfit for starting work.

"Mother!" Maggie was exasperated and tired. "You have tons of clothes in your closet. Wear one of those outfits." They had gone to six different stores and had no luck.

"No, it isn't right. This is way too short. Too expensive." Molly had one excuse after another for not buying what she tried on.

"No, I need something new and fashionable," Molly stated emphatically. "We'll try again tomorrow."

Sunday, Maggie invited Rose to go with them. "Be sure to wear comfortable shoes," her friend warned her.

142

In the end, it was Rose who picked out the perfect ensemble for her 'second' mom. It was a pretty jade green skirt. The top was a leafy print made up of the same green, plus a lighter one, some yellow and daubs of red here and there. With the belt to match the lighter green, the outfit appeared to be one piece and was very becoming. The trio picked out a gold chain necklace with matching earrings to complete the fashion. It only took three shoe stores before the entire outfit was complete.

"Now I can go to work in style." Her satisfied smile caused the girls to laugh.

"Mom, you're acting just like a teenager going on a first date." Maggie was thrilled to see her mom this enthusiastic about life.

Feigning indignation, Molly whined, "Well, you don't want me to look like a perfect slob, do you? One never knows who one will meet in my business."

The three shoppers were laughing hysterically when the waitress arrived with their food. The giggles quickly abated as they dove into their burgers and fries. All in all it turned out to be a wonderful day. On Monday, as everyone in the office welcomed Molly, each one commented on how beautiful she looked.

It didn't take the woman long to fall back into the routine. Even some of her old clients remembered her and welcomed her back.

"I guess it's like riding a bike," she expressed to Pat one afternoon. "Once you have the skill, you never lose it."

Pat just chuckled and waved on her way to her own office. She considered Molly to be the whiz of all caterers and was very glad to have those talents working for her again. Pat confided to Sophie one day, "I sure am glad Molly's not working for the competition. I'd be out of business."

In truth, Molly loved the work. It was rewarding, fulfilling and a lot of fun. Her creativity was always being challenged as she arranged dinner parties and receptions galore.

She kept a photo album of all the different themes she had used, along with some she would love to try. Her favorite photo depicted the time she set up and served a New England seafood feast, lobster being the main course, to a group of Japanese dignitaries. The affair was sponsored by Webster Computer Company for their foreign investors. The building's dining area was decorated with lobster traps, fishing nets, and buoys, and all guests were given a yellow Gloucester fisherman's hat to wear for the festivities.

"Gloucester is a fishing town on the northeastern shore of Massachusetts," the company president explained to the guests. "In the harbor stands a statue of a fisherman manning the wheel of his vessel wearing a hat resembling the ones children wore with their bright yellow slickers on rainy days, just like the ones given to you." The day after the feast, all the visitors boarded a bus to visit Gloucester to view the famous statue.

Molly and her crew of servers, laughed for days over fond memories of the Japanese dignitaries trying to eat the boiled lobster placed in front of them. Her photo depicteded said men and women, complete with white plastic bibs, cracking the shells of the red crustaceans.

Sophie continued to work for the Stelson women, coming in three days a week. However, Molly made it a point to be home when Maggie came in from school as often as she could. Her now five foot tall and growing child was much more relaxed and excelling in her final years of elementary school. She and Rose were inseparable and if one wasn't at the other's house they were talking on the phone.

"Mother, *please*," Maggie responded once when Molly had the gall to ask what she and Rose had to talk about since they only left each other thirty minutes earlier.

Because of the girls' friendship, Molly and Denise were becoming good friends in their own right. Maggie would often tell Molly she worried too much so Mol would ask Denise if Maggie's behavior was normal.

"Believe me!" Denise Arlton would exclaim. "It's normal!"

Three days after Maggie turned twelve, she and Rose graduated with their class from sixth grade. They would be heading for junior high in the fall, and were already discussing possible adventures they may or may not experience.

Denise and Molly surprised the pair with a four-day trip to New York City. After much packing and repacking, the four of them left on the morning train. It actually turned out to be three days of touring and two days of traveling but none of the women seemed to care. They had a fabulous time. In those three days they managed to take a boat ride around the Statue of Liberty, rode to the top of the Empire State Building, visited the United Nations, the RCA building, and Radio City Music Hall. They also saw Rockerfeller Center, went window shopping in Saks Fifth Avenue, explored Broadway and Times Square, took mounds of pictures, ate a lot and thoroughly enjoyed New York City. All four slept the entire train ride home. In fact, they had to be awakened by the conductor when they reached their stop. Rose and Maggie talked about the trip for weeks afterward. Molly and Denise were glad their gift was a hit with the girls.

Molly continued to see Linda but had "graduated" to every three months. Molly knew she was better when she almost forgot her March appointment.

"I remember," she told her shrink, "when I used to live for my appointments. Now I almost forget to come."

Linda was extremely proud of her patient and loved listening to Molly's stories each visit. Mol was making up for the thirty years she survived but never really lived. Her doctor just smiled and nodded - she also remembered those days.

Junior high proved a pleasant experience for both girls. They were together for some classes and thrilled about that. They spent hours comparing teachers of those subjects where they were separated.

"Mr. Swadson is fair but strict," Rose stated about her science teacher.

"Yeah - well so's Ms. Owens, and she makes things fun."

145

"Oh, yeah?" Rose would retort. "You should see my French instructor. He is *soooo* cute."

Their parents got a kick out of the criteria by which they judged their teachers.

"Rose is getting so boy-crazy," Denise confided in her friend. "Her concentration on her studies is lacking. Her notebook looks like one of those trees all the kids carve. You know - all those hearts containing initials, R.A. loves M.K. an so on. She's my first teenage girl. I hope I'm up for the challenge."

Maggie didn't seem to be into boys that much and Molly wondered why. However, every so often a boy would call and Maggie talked freely to him so Molly relaxed. "Maybe she's just too practical to get too 'boy-crazy," Mol told Sophie one day while the two planned dinner together.

A pretty girl, Mags did have boys around her a lot. She liked them enough but didn't want to get too close. She put up a wall if they tried to be boyfriend and not just friend. "You're going to say 'no' so many times they'll give up," Rose complained to her friend. "Why not give it a try? You know my mom won't let me go out unless I at least double date. Please say yes to Paul when he asks. Chris already asked me and we could go together. Please."

In the end, Maggie said yes for her friend's sake.

Friday night, Chris's dad drove the quartet to the movie theater and promised to pick them up at nine fifteen. To Maggie's pleasure, they actually had a wonderful time.

"I was really nervous," she told her mom later that night. "I don't know why now. It was a fun evening."

Molly smiled. Her little girl was growing up.

Now, a year and a half later, Molly was pulling together the menu for her "little girl's" sixteenth birthday party. Pat had, of course, offered to cater which did not surprise Molly at all. It had only taken the girls four mind changes and three arguments to agree on a menu. It was only when Mol pinned them down that they finally decided.

"Look, girls - I have to know by today at four if you want food for your party. If you can't agree you'll have to buy and cook your own. Now make up your minds!"

The pair entered Maggie's mom's office at three with a menu all written up.

"Here's what we'd like." Maggie handed the list to her mother. "Is that okay?"

Molly read the list. Pizza, chips, finger food - those little hot dogs, deviled eggs, etc.; cold cuts, cheese, rolls and whatever goes with these things, such as mayo, you know; and cake and ice cream.

"Very interesting list," Molly mumbled. "At least your guests will be well fed."

"Ah, mom," Rose nudged Maggie into speaking. "We wanted to tell you that we're sorry for taking so long and putting this off. Auntie Pat is so good to do this, just like you, and we should have been more considerate. We're really sorry."

"Yes, ma'am," Rose piped in, "We've been talking and are very sorry. We'll try to be more conscientious in the future."

"Girls, you have, for the most part, been wonderful about this and I can't complain. The only problem with the catering is that there have to be deadlines in order to have preparation time. You both have been very grown up these past few weeks. I'm proud of both of you. Now get out of here and let me do my work."

"Mom," Maggie ran around the desk to give her mom a big hug and kiss. "I sure do love you. I love you very, very much!"

Waving and giggling, the dynamic duo went bounding out. Mol was still smiling when Pat stuck her head in to say she had a meeting and would Molly please lock up.

"I'll be with a buyer most of tomorrow and another one on Friday. If I don't see you, I'll surely see you Saturday at the social affair of the century." Pat blew her employee a kiss and headed to Rochester. She sighed as she parked the car.

How I hate these things, she thought as she got out to face her obligations.

She had been talking to Sophie a great deal lately about retiring.

"I'm getting tired, darling." she'd complain "After all, I've been doing this for more years than I care to remember. I need to do something. I don't know what yet, but I want to retire."

Sophie had offered some suggestions and she herself had thought of a few. However, they hadn't come to any decisions. As Pat headed for the meeting room with her buyers, she thought again of how tired she was. All of a sudden an idea entered her mind.

I must remember to bounce this off Sophie tonight at supper, she told herself. Pat's step was much lighter when she greeted her buyers and walked to the head of the table.

Rose slept over at the Stelson's Friday night. The two friends talked far into the night reviewing all the plans and making sure they hadn't forgotten anything.

"Girls, it's one in the morning. If you don't get some sleep, you won't have enough energy to enjoy your own party. Lights out, now! Okay?"

" 'kay, Mom," the girls called out in stereo. "We're going to sleep, honest. Good night."

Molly walked back to her room, laughing to herself. She knew darn well they'd just talk with the lights out.

"They won't sleep much, tonight," she grinned. "How can I be stern and spoil their excitement?"

She turned off her light and went to sleep.

"They were up most of the night and going all day long," Molly told Denise that evening. "I can't believe their energy. Nice to be young."

"It is amazing, isn't it?" Denise replied. "I went through it with the boys but not to this extent. And I have two more to get through!" I hope I live to tell you about their antics when they're older." She just rolled her eyes and sighed.

"Well, while we're still young," Molly added, "What do you say we roll up our sleeves and lend a hand? The guests will be arriving soon."

An hour later the party was underway and turning out to be a big success. The adults stayed in the kitchen playing cards while the gang enjoyed the evening. Molly only had to get Maggie's attention once to ask her to turn the music down just a bit.

"We don't want to get arrested for disturbing the peace," she shouted.

Maggie rolled her eyes, "Oh, Mother, really!" However, she made her way to the stereo and brought the volume down.

"Now," Molly said to the group safely back in the kitchen. "Shall we take bets on how long it stays down?" They just laughed, remembering when they themselves were young.

Maggie wondered how long the doorbell had been ringing as she walked to the door. Until the last song ended she wasn't aware of the pealing chimes. Spotting her mom heading that way, she yelled, "I'll get it. It may be Randy. He went out a while ago to get more soda."

Mol waved and turned around and Mags grabbed the door knob. The door swung open and she turned to look. The young hostess stood there not knowing what to do. She felt rooted to the spot and stunned.

"Hi," he said.

149

Chapter Eighteen

Maggie couldn't believe her eyes, let alone speak.

He looked so awful. His hair was quite gray and thinning on top. What was left was uncombed and dirty. There were dark circles under his eyes, and the stubble on his face made it appear as if he hadn't shaved in days. His appearance was one of major dishevelment. His pants and shirt were wrinkled as if he had slept in them, his collar was open, and his stained tie hung loosely around his neck. He looked much older than his forty three years and there was a deep sadness in his gray eyes.

He spoke again, bringing Maggie out of her trance.

"Hi, princess, it's Dad. Don't you recognize me? You look beautiful tonight. Is your mom home?" He hoped his nervousness didn't come out in his voice. "Please, tell her I'm here. I really need to speak to her."

Maggie didn't know whether to feel pity or anger for the man at first. However, listening to him she could only feel rage at what he did to her and Mom.

"What are you doing here? How dare you show up like this. I hate you for running out on us, and so does Mom. Why don't you just go away!" She valiantly tried to hold back her tears.

"Maggie, what's taking you so -" Rose stopped in her tracks when she saw Jake.

"I'm comin', Rose. He's just leaving." To her estranged father she said, "I'll tell Mom to call you. Where will you be?"

Just then, Maggie felt a gentle hand on her shoulder. "It's okay, honey - go back to your guests." Molly spoke gently but firmly.

Mags disappeared into the other room and Molly motioned to Jake to go out on to the porch. They sat down on the two all-weather chairs opposite each other.

"Jake," Molly began calmly. "What are you doing here? How could you come back after all these years?"

"Molly, I needed to see you and Maggie." Looking toward the house, he continued. "She has turned into a beautiful young lady, hasn't she? You've done a good job, Mol." There was a noticeable sadness and longing in his voice. Molly was filled with pity for him. A spark she hadn't dared to feel in years seemed to rekindle within her. However, she was not going to let it surface.

It can never be, she told herself, adamantly. *Better to let sleeping dogs lie.*

"Did you know today is her sixteenth birthday? All her friends are here celebrating with her. She planned for weeks for this party. I don't want you going in and spoiling it for her.

"Where have you been, Jake? Where's Juliann? Did she dump you for a younger man?" Molly couldn't keep the sarcasm out of her voice. "Or did you come back to see if I was still sane and hadn't killed myself yet? You look terrible, you know? I would have thought your wife would have taken better care of you. After all, she's practically old enough to be your mother."

Jake Stelson started to cry. As the tears came Molly's anger turned to pity, and she put her arms around him and held him close. He just sobbed in her arms like a little boy.

Molly held him in silence about five minutes before he was able to regain his composure and sit up.

Much more calmly now, Molly said to the man she once loved, still loved. "Jake, what did happen?" she asked quietly.

Jake leaned forward. Looking down at his folded hands, he told her his story.

"When Juli and I moved to Detroit, we were totally on our own. Dad gave me the transfer with the understanding he never wanted to see me again. He was enraged because I was leaving you and marrying her.

" 'Your wife is sick, for Christ's sake! She needs your love and support, not this. You're a coward! Do you know that? If you do this foolish thing, you'll never be welcomed in this family again,' were his exact words to me," Jake groaned.

He spent the next hour or more explaining to his ex-wife the past six years which, to his regret, he spent without her.

The pair had arrived in Detroit tired and hungry. They had driven all night in the pouring rain. Then at six thirty in the morning, the only eating establishment open was a run-down looking Pancake Pavilion. However, it was clean and the food turned out to be delicious. Over coffee they discussed what they would do from there.

Jake had two days before he had to start work at the new branch of Stelson Computer Sales. That gave them time to find an apartment. They would look for a house later, and get somewhat settled.

James Stelson II never wanted to see his son again! He gave Jake a generous allowance and vowed to cut him from his will.

"At least he allowed me to keep my job." Jake was cynical. "How generous of him!"

A week after their arrival, the couple found a lovely three bedroom apartment in a one of the suburbs of Detroit. It was located in an apartment complex consisting of only eight buildings. The structures were only one story, so that all the apartments were side by side. Juliann liked that. The thought of people walking above her was appalling.

"We'll always be hearing them stomp around, drop things," she'd say. "I won't live with someone over me!"

The complex was well landscaped and quite pretty. It had a club house, pool, tennis courts, and gym. Their abode was spacious with plenty of closet space. Each room had a large window, so the apartment was sunny and pleasant. There were two bathrooms: one adjoining the master bedroom, and one between the other two bedrooms.

The kitchen was compact but big enough for them. There was a laundry area off the kitchen. There was a dining area beside the kitchen and a huge living room area.

Jake and Juli went out and bought a bedroom set, dinette set, and the rest of the furniture they picked up little by little. It turned out Juli had a talent for decorating, and by the following year the place was "home".

"After you gave me a divorce," Jake went on, "We made plans to be married. It was a small ceremony with only a few friends. Juli's family wanted no part of this 'ridiculous exploit', as they dubbed it. I could tell she was heartbroken, but she overcame the disappointment well."

The first two years of their marriage went well for Juliann and James Stelson. Both of them began to forget the past, or so they thought, and looked ahead. They both believed their love would sustain them through any difficulty. Jake was working hard and Juli became a secretary for a senior partner of a nearby law firm. They both agreed it would be a conflict of interests for her to work for him.

Juli let Jake go out with his friends often but never seemed interested in joining him.

"Come on," he'd coax. " We're going dancing. All the guys are bringing their wives. It'll be a lot of fun. Please, Jul."

"No, I'm too tired. You go have fun. I'll be okay here."

At first he'd go alone. He'd have a great time watching the dancers and drinking his vodka and tonic. Then after a while, he'd start thinking of Molly and how she loved to go places with him. She had been so full of energy and life. By the end of the evening, he'd be the one begging to sit and rest. Now he was so lonely and bored.

Soon, Jake began to make excuses to his friends why he couldn't go. He spent time with Juli, playing cards, or watching TV.

" 'What a life," he whined to his wife one night. "Can't you go out with me at least once in a while? I work hard all day just like you do. I don't see why you're always so wiped out.' "

" 'I'm older than you are, remember?' was her retort. 'I get tired faster. Plus, I don't enjoy the things you do.'

Then the arguments would begin.

Both adults began to realize that they weren't in love as they had thought. Jake had needed someone to care for him, and mistook the dependence and longing he felt for Juli as love. She was using him to replace the guilt she felt due to her late husband's death. Life in the apartment became unbearable for both. He started going out more and more, and she began eating more and sleeping a great deal.

"Finally," Jake continued, as Molly listened with pity and more love than she dared admit. "Two years ago I admitted I had made a mistake. I decided to divorce Juliann and come crawling back to you. I left work one Thursday, determined to talk to her that evening. But when I got home she was laying in bed moaning and crying. When I went over to her I realized she was very sick so I called 911. A half hour later we were in the emergency room. The following day her doctor called me at work and asked me to come into his office.

"I sat there stunned when he told me. 'Jake, your wife has cancer. It's in her right lung, and has spread to her stomach and abdomen. I'm afraid chemotherapy will do no good now. We can do some radiation to shrink it, a little, but more for relief than cure.'

" 'H-h-h-ow long?' I whispered, 'Before she...' I couldn't even say the words.

" 'I'd guess within a year,' he said, 'However, one can never say exactly.'

"Mol, I couldn't leave her then. She had no one. I tried calling her children, but they wouldn't return my calls. Eventually I had to leave work and stay with her. Luckily, I had invested the money Dad had given me, so financially we didn't have to worry. I hired some help for nights, so I could sleep, but I still tossed around most nights. She lasted two years and five days. When she died last Wednesday, she weighed sixty five pounds.

"The funeral was yesterday and - would you believe - not one of her children came? God, Molly- watching her die that slow painful death was a living hell. Her cries for her children, her loneliness, made me realize how much I loved you and Maggie.

"After the funeral, I made arrangements with the manager of our place to rent the apartment as is. I took nothing, except a few personal items, my clothes, and left. I drove straight here, only stopping for a few hours to sleep. I only did that because I just missed swerving into an oncoming truck when I dozed off behind the wheel. The driver blew the whistle just in time for me to maneuver out of the way. I pulled over to the shoulder and slept in the car for a few hours.

"Molly, I know I don't deserve anything from you," Jake's voice was pleading. "But I had nowhere else to go. Can you find it in your heart to forgive me, and take me back? I never stopped loving you, Molly - never!"

Chapter 19

"No, Mom - don't do it!" came the adamant voice of their sixteen year old daughter. "Can't you see he's snowing you? All he wants is a place to stay, a free ride. He's not worth it, Mom. He'll just hurt us again. Please, Mom - don't give in!"

Molly could see the rage and hurt in Maggie's eyes as she turned to face the youth. "How long have you been standing there?" She didn't mean to sound so cross. "This is a private conversation. You're eavesdropping." Unable to curb her disappointment, Maggie began to cry. Molly heard the agony in her child's sobs and her heart broke. *How could I be so unfeeling as to respond that way?* Molly thought as she jumped up to embrace her teen. "I'm sorry darling, I shouldn't have been so harsh with you."

As she comforted Maggie, Molly remembered the party. "Oh, Mags, is it time to cut the cake?" Molly reached for the door handle.

"Don't bother, Mother." Maggie's voice was full of sarcasm. "The party broke up fifteen minutes ago. Everybody's gone." She continued in sadness. "I came looking for you when it was time to blow out the candles. When I saw you with him, I didn't interrupt. 'Mom' Arlton realized what was going on, and brought in the dessert. I blew out the candles - but obviously, didn't get my wish - and opened the gifts. By the way, I suppose I should say thank you for the skirt, sweater, the accessories and the money. It was very sweet of you!" The sarcasm was back in her voice. "We all sat or stood around in the dining room and kitchen, after that. No one dared come back in the living room. I think they were afraid they might hear something. If you think no one noticed, you're wrong. Anyway, after about half an hour, people started drifting away. They all went out the side door and through the garage, so as not to disturb your little tete-a- tete.

"When the kids had all gone, Rose left with her mom. Sophie, Aunt Pat and I started to clean up, but didn't have the desire, so we just left everything as it was. I gave them each a big hug and walked them to the car. I'm becoming used to it. This is probably time number one hundred when the two of them were there for me, when it should have been the two of you."

"When I came back in, after they drove away, I noticed you still talking, and came in to listen. Yes, Mother, Father." Maggie looked them square in the eyes, first one, then the other. "Yes, I listened on purpose. And you know - I don't care. I just don't care! I guess, deep down inside, I knew something would happen to spoil this evening. It was just too good to be true." She couldn't stop the hurt from replacing the sarcasm in her voice as the evidence of it streamed down her face.

Molly held her teenager closely, and gently stroked her hair. "Sweetheart, we didn't mean to..."

Mags interrupted. "No, you never mean to!" She pulled away from her mother, screaming at her parents, turned and fled back into the house.

All this time Jake sat quietly, not knowing what to say or do. It was his fault, it all was, and he knew it, yet he couldn't make himself say it aloud. Molly's voice startled him, interrupting his ruminating.

"I have to go to her," Molly said almost inaudibly and headed toward the door.

"Mol," Jake looked at her pleadingly. "What about my request?" He realized by the way she glared at him it was not the right thing to say, but he had to. His tense body relaxed when she responded.

"You can sleep in the guest room for tonight," she said flatly. "I need time to think about the rest."

She followed Maggie up the stairs. She knocked a number of times, with no response. Finally, Molly decided Maggie was not going to answer and tried the knob. The door was locked. "I'm so sorry, honey," she whispered to the barrier between them. Molly went to bed knowing a sleepless night was ahead of her.

Molly Stelson looked at the clock on her bedside table. Four o'clock. Sure enough, she had been tossing and turning for hours. Trying to get out of bed, Molly had to untangle herself from her sheets. Her bed was as messed up as her mind seemed to be.

Four and a half hours earlier, Mol took a long, cool shower, crawled in between the sheets and began to sort out this new development in her life. Trying to remember the tools Linda had taught her over the years, she mulled over Jake's request without success. As the hours slowly passed, Molly found herself becoming increasingly frustrated at not finding a solution. Finally she consciously chose to put it out of her head, vowing to call Linda in the morning. Her shrink could always make her see things more clearly. Molly had the idea that having decided that, she'd sleep. Wrong! She tried so hard not to think about it that it haunted her.

Seeing the hour hand on the four, Molly knew it was ridiculous to stay in bed any longer. She donned a robe and slippers and headed downstairs. Molly made a pot of fresh coffee, poured herself a cup, and sat down at the kitchen table to continue her deliberations. She hadn't been there long when she heard footsteps behind her and turned quickly.

"May I join you?" Jake asked awkwardly. Not getting any reply, he poured himself a mugful and sat opposite his former wife."I take it you couldn't sleep, either?" He tried to make conversation as her silence was bothering him. Finally, he heard, "Did you expect me to?" She didn't even look up. "Most men leave their wives for younger women. You left me for an older one." Turning in her chair so she could rest on one elbow, Molly continued. "With no support from you, I got my life together, and built up a wonderful relationship with our daughter. Things were going along smoothly and she was happy. So was I, for that matter! Now, suddenly, you show up out of the blue and ask to come back. What did you think I was going to do last night? Dream happy thoughts?"

"Mol, please believe me when I say I didn't come back to hurt you or Maggie. I was wrong to leave you. I never stopped loving you both. Even Juliann noticed that. We had talked about it often, and I was planning to leave her and come back to you. I had even talked to a lawyer about an amicable divorce."

He paused to see the disbelief in her eyes. He continued more emphaically. "Right at the same time I admitted to myself I needed to return to you, Juli became sick. Then I felt too guilty to leave. I was all she had."

Reaching across the table, he placed his hand on hers. "Molly, if you can honestly tell me you have no feeling left for me, I'll leave and never come back. I promise. "

Molly looked at her ex- husband with tear- filled eyes. "I can't tell you that," she whispered.

Jake's voice softened. "Do you think we could start over, try again?"

Molly could not speak, nor could she pull away. She knew that she still loved him.

Eventually, feeling more at ease, he got up and fixed them a big breakfast, consisting of toast, bacon, and his specialty of ham, cheese, and onion omelets. They began to relax with each other, and reminisce about the happy times they had spent together.

When Maggie got up and dressed, arriving at the kitchen door, she could hear her parents talking and laughing together. Disgusted, she slipped out the front door and headed for Rose's house. She walked the two miles only to find the Arltons not home. At the sight of the empty driveway, Maggie remembered her friend saying the family was leaving early Sunday morning to visit her great-aunt.

"Tomorrow, we're going to drive to Connecticut to visit Aunt Ethel," Rose said, full of excitement. "We'll be gone only a week. By then Auntie's had enough of us and sends us packing." Rose giggled. Maggie was as excited for Rose as Rose was. She felt as if she knew Rose's aunt just by listening to all the stories her pal told her.

The way Rose described her great aunt reminded Maggie of a movie she once saw starring Lucille Ball, called "Mame".

When Mags returned home sometime later, Molly was waiting for her, and invited Maggie to sit. The two of them rocked in silence on the same porch swing that Molly shared with Jake the previous evening.

"Maggie." Molly finally broke the silence. She spoke firmly to her daughter yet as gently as possible. "I have decided to give your dad a second chance."

Not even looking up Mags simply said, "I figured you would." There was no mistaking the disappointment in her voice.

Molly continued before her courage left her.

"Sweetie, I never stopped loving him. I thought I had. I believed I had let go of him and the past. But seeing him again last night, I knew I hadn't. I think I have always blamed myself for pushing him away. Don't you see? This is a second chance for me, for *all* of us." She was pleading for Maggie to understand.

"No, I don't see!" Maggie yelled back. "He's just going to hurt us again. How can you believe him? How can you trust him?"

"Mags." She stroked her daughter's long, dark hair. "I need to try. I called Linda earlier, and we talked quite a while before I decided. Jake has agreed to go to joint counseling with me. That tells me he is willing to try. You are welcome to come with us to Linda's as well. Please, darling- I know it won't be easy, and it may not work, but I have to try. I don't know if I can explain why to your satisfaction, but I need to do this. You have a right to your own feelings. I respect that. Even if you don't agree with me, please respect my feelings, my decision."

"Mom." Maggie spoke softly as she heard the sincerity in her mother's voice. "It's your life. If you want to risk ruining it now and letting him hurt you again, fine. But that doesn't mean I have to. I really mean this: I hope it works for you, I do. However, I don't know if I can ever love him again."

Before her mother could respond, Maggie got up and went up to her room. She felt so betrayed again. She couldn't figure out what was going on inside of her. *How come she can forgive him and I can't?* she thought to herself. *After all, his leaving hit her harder than it did me.* At that moment, she realized more strongly than ever just how much she missed Rose, her friend and confidant.

To Maggie's surprise, things went pretty smoothly those first few weeks. Jake did as he promised and went with Molly to see Linda. He and Mol were both so happy that it began to rub off on Maggie. She started letting her defenses down and joining in the family more. *Maybe, he's really changed,* she thought. *Maybe we can finally be a real family.* These thoughts ran through her head as she watched her dad put his arm around Molly. Her parents sat on the couch laughing at some old black and white movie with a bowl of popcorn in front of them. She wondered at how much of the movie they were seeing. It really was nice to see them together that way. Since the movie didn't appeal to her, Mags decided to let them be alone. She kissed them both good night and went up to bed.

Exactly two nights later, Molly had to supervise the catering staff at a fancy affair celebrating some couple's silver wedding anniversary. They were very important clients and it was she who brought them through every step to get to that night. She had to see it through to completion. Molly's face just lit up when Jake asked if he could accompany her. Maggie looked up from her book when she heard them on the stairs and smiled. "I bet you'll be the best looking couple there," she beamed. Her dad looked very handsome in his navy blue suit and starched white shirt. Her mom looked like Cinderella heading for the ball. "Mom, make sure he brings you home before midnight or you'll turn into a pumpkin." Maggie laughed along with her parents.

It was a little after six when her parents pulled out of the driveway. When the car turned the corner, Maggie went inside and fixed herself supper. She cleaned up her dishes and went to watch TV for a while, then headed upstairs. Soon she was curled up in bed with a good book. It was early, about nine thirty when she heard a knock at her bedroom door. She didn't have time to respond.

"Princess, may I come in?" Her dad stuck his head in the room. "I just wanted to say good night." He walked over to the bed. "Mom had to do some finishing up stuff. One of her staff offered to drive her home, so I left. She told me it would be boring for me to wait around for her.

"I was heading for bed and saw your light. I wanted to thank you again for accepting me back and being so gracious these last three months. I know you were against it in the beginning." He sat on the bed and began running his fingers through her long tresses. Without warning, he laid down beside her on the bed and she cringed. His hand began to fondle her breasts and run down her. When she tensed up, he told her to relax. For some reason, she couldn't stop him from touching her, even though she knew it was wrong. When he left, a half hour later, she felt so guilty and ashamed. Why did she let him do that?

Maggie had forgotten the past, so didn't realize the power he had over her. Somewhere deep in her subconscious she heard those words again. *It's your fault, you know. You're bad. If you tell anyone, you'll die and go to hell. Besides, no one will believe you, anyway.* That night, the confused, shame-filled daughter of Jake and Molly Stelson curled up into a fetal position and cried herself to sleep.

Chapter Twenty

"I just don't understand, Mom," Rose shared her concerns while helping Denise prepare dinner. "Maggie has been so distant and quiet lately. She seems like she's gone back to the way she was when I first met her. It's like the life has gone out of her."

"Rosie, maybe she's just having a hard time adjusting to her dad being back. Give her time, darling. Be there for her if she needs to talk or whatever, but let her have her space."

"I guess you're right," Rose shrugged. "I still worry about her. Oh, well - I'll try to be patient. I'm so glad I have you to bounce things around with. Thanks, Ma." She gave her mom a great big hug and went on with her peeling.

Rose was right in her judgment: since Jake came home three months before, Maggie was withdrawing more and more. Molly noticed it as well. She chalked it up to the change in Mags' world and hoped her daughter would soon accept her dad.

Jake was being so good to both of them. He was true to his word and went with his wife once a week to see Linda. They were dealing with a lot of denial and anger inside both of them, yet they were making progress and Molly's love for her husband was deepening. He worked as a consultant for his dad's firm and did a great deal of work out of the home. Most days he was there when Maggie came home from school which made Molly feel a lot better.

Shortly after Maggie's sixteenth birthday, Sophie decided to retire. Her lawyer had helped her to invest her inheritance wisely and she was able to live off the interest alone and quite comfortably. They were sorry to see her go but understood her need. Molly arranged and supervised the catering of a lovely party celebrating the thirteen years she had been a part of the Stelson household. The housekeeper was thrilled by how much people cared about her. She couldn't believe the number of people who came to the party.

Maggie insisted she was old enough to be home alone, but Molly still worried about her being in the house by herself. She was relieved when Jake said he'd be home most afternoons.

As the year progressed Maggie went off by herself a great deal or spent many days over at Rose's.

"I just have a lot of homework, that's all," she quickly responded when Molly commented that she seemed to be avoiding her family.

"Maggie, honey," Molly chided her, "Dad's trying *so* hard to make us a family again. Can't you give a little, also? You never want to do anything with us anymore. Try, please - for me."

Finally Molly gave up and tried to appease Jake by telling him she was just growing up. It was a phase.

January of her junior year, Maggie spent two weeks with Sophie and Aunt Pat. Her parents decided to go on a second honeymoon, which was fine with her. Sophie and Pat were more than happy to have her and one of them would drive her to school each day.

The first Saturday she was with them, Sophie and Pat took her shopping at the new Mall in downtown Buffalo.

"It has a hundred stores," Pat chortled, "You'll just love it."

Later, the trio plopped down at their table in the food court gratefully. Surrounded by parcels, they began devouring their pepperoni pizza.

"Look, Aunt Pat," Maggie suddenly whispered to the woman sitting beside her. "That group over there - I think they're deaf."

Pat looked over to see the hands flying and nodded to her adopted niece. "Yes - they're from The Buffalo School for the Deaf. It's only a few blocks from here. Some of the kids board there during the year."

Maggie couldn't help but to watch them in awe. She began to wonder what it must be like never to hear anything. Did they miss music? How did they get up in the morning without hearing an alarm clock? What about talking with people who could hear? All the way home she talked about how hard it must be for them and how sorry she felt for them.

"I wish somehow I could do something to help," Maggie confided to Sophie that night as her former caretaker helped her make up her bed. Sophie and Pat had long since moved into one bedroom.

"Look," Pat said. "Why don't you take tomorrow off and I'll take you over to visit the school. Maybe they'll let you take a tour and I'm sure they can answer your questions better than we can."

Maggie couldn't sleep that night, due to her excitement. She had called Rose to tell her the news. "Take good notes in class and I'll tell you all about my adventure on Tuesday."

By Monday evening, Maggie had decided to become a teacher of the Deaf. The school was marvelous and she wanted to be a part of the Deaf world. She had learned that Deaf didn't just mean a hearing loss but a way of life, a culture. "To teach Deaf children, " the school counselor informed her, "is no different than teaching hearing children, except you need to use a different language."

"I thought sign language was just abbreviated English," Maggie questioned. "Isn't it?"

"Oh no," the woman went on, " American Sign Language, or ASL, is a language in its own right. In fact it's the third largest, non-English language in the United States."

Maggie left the school with answers to many of her questions and brochures and pamphlets galore. Mrs. Trent, her guide and informer, told her of many schools which taught Deaf Education, the Community College in Buffalo being one of them.

"I probably should stay loyal to New York," she whispered to Maggie. "But the program with the best reputation on the east coast is Boston University. It's supposed to be one of the best."

Maggie worked very hard the rest of her junior year and into her senior year to keep her grades up and read as much as she could about the Deaf culture and ASL. She even got a book and taught herself the alphabet and some basic signs. Both she and Rose did very well on the SAT's and talked endlessly about college.

Rose had decided to go into business administration and minor, of all things, in philosophy. She wanted someday to join her father in his business which was growing all the time. He had recently opened a second shop and told her he would let her run it when she was ready.

"I figure the philosophy may give me some insight into how people think and help me with my business," Rose said deviously.

"You are a nut." Maggie could only laugh at her best friend's logic.

September of their senior year both girls applied to Boston University. Much to Molly's chagrin, Maggie would not apply anywhere else. "What if you don't get accepted?" her mom kept asking.

"Mom, drop it, will you?" Maggie said rather harshly. "It's my life and I'll do things the way I want."

Molly walked away with a sigh. *We used to be able to talk*, she thought to herself. *What has happened to make my child so irritable?*

During the past two years since Jake's return, he had been visiting Maggie's room at least once a month. Sometimes he'd want to "love her" when she came home from school. Mostly, though, it was on nights Molly had to work late. Maggie hated those nights and tried everything. "I don't feel good." "I have my period." "I'm spending the night at Rose's." Despite her protestations, he still managed to get to her quite frequently. She would just lay there and wait for him to finish and dream of the day she could leave home and never come back.

Rose heard from Boston University first. She waited for Maggie to hear before she accepted and finally three weeks later, her friend's letter arrived, telling Maggie she had been accepted.

The two pals embraced and danced around the room. From that day on, they planned what they would do as college roommates. It was going to be wonderful.

Maggie was especially happy. She could get away from the abuse she was experiencing. She had been able to tell no one, not even her dearest friend, what her father was doing. Now it would end forever. She longed for September.

Both girls had graduated with honors, worked hard all summer and were constantly shopping for college. Fall finally came and the duo began their freshman year at Boston University.

Molly had developed quite a bad cold early in September, which seemed to just hang on, so Fred and Denise offered to drive the "college kids" to Massachusetts. Jake was grateful as he felt his place was with Molly. Maggie was thrilled with the arrangements, though she worried about her mother. She had never seen Molly so thin and pale.

Maggie loved her work and was kept very busy. Rose struggled at first but finally seemed to reach a satisfactory routine. Her classes were rigorous and sometimes quite difficult. Schoolwork, up until now, had always come easily for Rose so when she got a D+ on her first exam she was ready to quit. However, she pulled it up on the second test and all of a sudden things clicked into place and she relaxed.

The food on campus was awful so the dynamic duo began to frequent the local fast food places. "I think I'm going to turn into a pizza soon," Rose laughed. It was the third night in a row they ended up at Pizza Heaven. Maggie laughed at the thought of sharing a room with a pizza and the two decided that they'd try Mexican the next night.

After Rose's last exam, the girls boarded an Amtrak heading home for Christmas. Maggie had all her papers and handed her final one in the day before. The freshmen were due to arrive home about six in the evening and Jake and Molly would be there to meet the train. Walking into the station, Maggie spotted her dad, who waved across the terminal.

He kissed her lightly on the cheek, greeted Rose and picked up the suitcases.

"Where's Mom?" Maggie asked as they walked to the parking area.

"She's been a little tired and run down so decided to wait at home," Jake said. "I think she's been trying to do too much with

169

work and all. She's been rushing around all week getting things ready for your homecoming. Once she relaxes for a few days, she'll be okay. Nothing to worry about."

Mags and Rose giggled and talked all the way home in the back seat. Maggie had to say hi to the Arltons so offered to help Rose with her luggage. Also, she was afraid to be alone with Jake.

Father and daughter entered the house filled with the fragrance of fresh baked cookies. The tree was set up in the front room, but was empty of decorations.

Molly came down from upstairs with outstretched arms to greet her only child. "Maggie, you look wonderful. I loved your letters - thank you. Come sit down and tell me all about college life."

Maggie thought her mother looked terrible. She was thin and pale and had black circles under her eyes. "Mom, are you okay? You look awfully tired." Maggie sounded worried.

"I'm okay, honey. I just try to do too much. The shop is keeping me busy since Pat is semi-retired. There's always something to do around here. You know me - I can't sit still for long."

"Shouldn't you go to a doctor to be sure?" Maggie continued. "Maybe he could give you some vitamins or something?"

"As a matter of fact," Mrs. Stelson retorted, "I have an appointment for a physical right after the holidays. So will you stop worrying and let's enjoy the vacation? We waited for you so we could decorate the tree. Sophie and Pat are coming for Christmas dinner and we are invited to the Arltons Christmas night. Now, why don't you go and unpack, then come help me with supper? I started it when Dad left for the station so we could eat as a family. Now scoot."

Maggie felt better hearing her mother's cheery disposition but felt something was wrong.

"No, you are not going to spend this vacation worrying," she reprimanded herself. By the time she returned to the kitchen Maggie was smiling and spent most of the meal filling her parents in on the trials and tribulations of campus life.

For the first time in a long time the three of them laughed together and enjoyed each other as a real family.

Chapter Twenty-One

Second semester went a little bit smoother for Mutt and Jeff, as they were affectionately known. They both began to fall into the groove of college life. Dorm life was not the ideal for the budding scholars as every night there seemed to be a party of some sort. Maggie and Rose had to lock the door many times so some smart-ass wouldn't drag them away from their studies.

"Come on. Where's your sense of fun?" the delegated escort would tease. "You can study tomorrow. College isn't supposed to be all work, you know?"

The two had begun to talk about moving off campus. However, the rule was that you had to be at least a sophomore before you could live off campus. For now all they could do was lock the door, don their ear plugs, and do their best to ignore the ribbings they took for being "nerdy bookworms".

The young women were thrilled when midterms were held that March. Evidently, reality hit their fellow students, and the many celebrations began to fade out a bit. "They probably got a good look at their grade point averages and panicked," Rose laughed. Both of the "nerdy bookworms" were pulling As in their classes.

"Maybe we should have a party and celebrate," quipped Maggie, causing the pair to roar with laughter.

Things went smoothly for the duo after midterms as the number of parties reduced drastically. Then one morning, Maggie returned from the library to find a message taped to her door. All it said was: "Call home." Knowing her parents never called here,

Mags grew more and more anxious as she ran upstairs, dumped her books on her bed, and headed for the phone.

Five minutes later, she was back in the room, throwing some things into a suitcase. Suddenly, Rose bounded in from her late afternoon class, and stopped dead when she noted Maggie's frantic packing.

"Mags, what's up?" queried her roommate nervously. "My mom's in the hospital," Maggie said, without looking up. "My dad's on his way here to pick me up. He should be here within the hour. Sophie was at the house waiting for me to return her call."

"Oh, Maggie, I'm sorry. Is it serious? Do you want me to come with you?" Rose ran to grab what she thought Maggie might need from the bathroom.

"No, it's okay. Sophie said Mom had pneumonia and was receiving antibiotics intravenously. She seemed a lot better today. I guess she went in last night. Rose." She turned to face her best buddy. "Mom looked so awful at Christmas time; I can't help thinking there's something they're not telling me. Do you think it could be cancer?"

Rose sat beside her on the bed. "Sophie is probably right. Don't jump to any conclusions. You're most likely worrying for nothing. Come on. Pneumonia can wear you down, too. Maggie, please, don't let your imagination run wild."

About forty minutes later, Rose waved to her friend as Maggie and her Dad headed home. "Please, God, let everything be okay."

Mags promised to call her when she knew anything, but Rose knew they wouldn't even arrive home until early the next morning. She didn't count on getting the call until the next evening. Trying not to worry, she focused her attentions on the work she had due the following day, then took a long hot bath and crawled into bed early. To her chagrin, Rose still had a restless night, due to worrying about her best friend.

Wednesday afternoon, Maggie was in Room 328 at Buffalo Memorial Hospital, sitting with her mother, who was pale and groggy. However, to Maggie's pleasant surprise, Molly looked better than the last time her daughter had seen her.

"It was pneumonia which I had let go too long. The doctor says I'm going to be okay in about a week. I'm eating better, sleeping a lot, and the medicine is helping. So, don't worry, darling. Sit here and tell me all about college."

Maggie felt a little better after she saw her mom, and when she called Rose that evening was able to relay positive news.

"I knew Sophie wouldn't lie." The relief Rose heard was evident. "How are you doing? Are you okay?"

"Yeah." Maggie sounded drained. "I'm okay. I'll stay here a few days and try to get back by Tuesday. Mom is supposed to come home on Monday if all goes well. Please, do me a favor, and tell Dr. Roberts. He'll get word to my other profs."

"Sure, and you get some rest, too. Don't you get sick, you hear?"

Maggie hung up the phone laughing. Her friend could be such a mother hen at times.

Molly came home as planned but she didn't seem all that happy to be there. Jake helped her settle on the couch, then, clearing his throat, announced he had to go out for a while. He left shortly thereafter.

Maggie sensed something was going on, and came over to sit with her mom on the couch.

"Is everything all right?" she asked. "Are things okay between you and Dad?" She could not hide the nervousness in her voice. Even though she had not agreed with her mother that taking her dad back would work, Maggie had to admit the past three years had been wonderful for her mom. She could tell the two adults were very much in love. Her mother seemed happier than ever.

"Sweetheart sit down. I have some things I want to tell you. I have already talked to your father and he agreed that you and I should be alone. I explained that I preferred to talk to you without him being present.

173

Maggie felt the color drain from her face. Her persistent fears of the past week filled her mind now. "Do you have cancer?" Her words sounded so far away.

"No, nothing like that," Molly was quick to reassure her. She turned away for a minute, coughed weakly, and faced her daughter again. "I had a strand of pneumonia called Legionnaires. It is a bacterial pneumonia rather than viral and can be quite serious. By the time I finally went to the doctor, I had it in both lungs and was very sick. He put me in the hospital immediately and began treatment. I guess I am lucky to be here, as this form of pneumonia can be fatal.

"Yesterday, when he came to discharge me, Dr. Smith told me I will be tired and weak for quite a while but eventually would be fine. Then, curiously, he turned to Jake, smiled, and said all tests were negative. I saw Jake heave a sigh of relief and blurted out, 'What?'

"Mags, Legionnaires is very common among HIV patients. Jake told me that Dr. Smith had approached him the day I was admitted, suggesting I be tested for HIV. I think the look on my face, at that moment, conveyed Jake's fears because he was by my side in an instant. Both he and the doctor assured me I did not have AIDS."

Maggie felt herself relax as her mother continued.

"At first I wasn't so sure. I didn't know a lot about the disease except how it is transmitted. I went on to tell your dad and Dr. Smith what I am about to tell you now. Please try to listen and not interrupt until I have finished. Can you do that for me?

"You never knew your Uncle Phil, my oldest brother. He died of AIDS when you were a baby. You see, he was gay. Evidently his significant other was carrying the virus and gave it to Phil.

"Maggie, from the time I was four - at least, that's as early as I can remember - Phil sexually abused me. No one knew because I couldn't talk about it. I was afraid. He had told me it was my fault and I was bad. I was filled with shame and guilt.

"When I was five, Phil went to college and every time he came back he would touch me more. But he was different. I guess that was where he met Tony, but I'm not sure. Anyway, Phil transferred to Salem State after two years and lived at home. At that time, he would come to my room a lot. He would touch my genitals, and even lick and kiss them. Sometimes he would make me touch and kiss his penis. Then, when I was eight, Maggie, he raped me. He penetrated me and had intercourse with an eight-year-old child. I was mortified and ashamed. For many years I believed it was my fault. There was something wrong with me.

"This treatment continued until I was almost twelve. I was ecstatic when my folks got tired of his slovenly behavior and threw Phil out of the house. However, by then I had become withdrawn, angry, and bitter. His actions have affected me all of my life.

"One night, shortly after Phil moved in with Tony, I tried telling your grandfather what had been happening, and guess what he did? He slapped me across the face. He called me a liar and informed me he would not let me make up such stories about his son, and if it did happen, that I must have brought it on myself.

"I had an extremely hard time trusting anyone after that. I built a wall around myself that no hurt could get through. It worked until I met your father. He made me laugh, and feel again. I was like a little kid living life for the first time.

"He used to laugh at the way I would get excited at simple pleasures. I fell head over heels in love with him, and we had a storybook marriage. Except I had not dealt with my past, only suppressed it, making myself forget.

"Linda explained to me that all the hurt and betrayal I had kept at arm's length all those years surfaced when I lost my first two babies, and then your twin sister. I just couldn't cope with anymore hurt, which is why I gave in to depression and withdrawal. My suicide attempts were calls for help, and finally Linda was there to listen. Your dad leaving us was the final straw, and something in me snapped. Luckily, instead of a renewed desire to kill myself, I developed a strong desire to fight back.

"It was Dr. Strong, a colleague of Linda's, who helped me remember. He had a special treatment, which helped me remember, and in remembering I could feel the pain, and in feeling it I could let it go. It would no longer come back to haunt me.

"After that week from hell, my life was worth living again. I was no longer afraid; I knew I could cope. I was given a new beginning and the past few years have been wonderful. Now I've had to face it all again.

"Maggie, when I finished my story, your dad just held me in his arms and we wept together. He was so understanding, not judging or condemning. I feel so relieved right now. For so long I blamed myself and felt ashamed, frightened that you and your dad would find out. I no longer have secrets, the past can no longer hurt me."

Molly saw the pain in her daughter's face, reached over and held her close. "Darling, I love you and I'm sorry to have to tell you this. Please don't feel bad for me."

Molly stopped talking and took a deep breath. Maggie found the silence unbearable, but could say nothing. Her face was soaked and she realized she had been sobbing the whole time her mom was relating this God awful story.

"Mommy." Maggie put her arms around her mom and held on tight. "How can people do those things to the people they love? It's so cruel!"

Mother and daughter held each other for a long time. It was as if they were afraid to let each other go. A few minutes earlier, Jake had tiptoed in, saw them, and went quietly up to bed. If they had seen him they gave no indication.

On Tuesday, the three Stelsons moved about as if one loud noise would cause their world to end. Breakfast was eaten in silence. When she finished, Mags went upstairs to get her things together for her train ride back to Boston. Molly had convinced her that it would be better for her to return to college. "The doctor said it could be years before I come down with AIDS. He has given me vitamins and a strict regimen to keep healthy, so it won't do you any good to stay around and worry. You be better off studying and keeping yourself busy."

Reluctantly, an hour later, Maggie kissed her folks good-bye, and boarded the train.

Chapter Twenty-Two

The train ride back to school proved a nightmare for Maggie. The young woman had nothing to do, and nowhere to go to escape her thoughts and feelings.

Why? Why do people do those things? Life is just so unfair.

She tried to imagine what life must have been like for her mother growing up. How she admired the woman for coping and surviving all the pain. Maggie never realized how brave her mom was, until this point. *You sure did endure a lot, Mom,* Maggie spoke from her heart. *I hope I can always be as courageous as you are.*

Molly's story echoed again and again in Maggie's head. Suddenly tears streamed down her face again as she realized that since he came back, Dad had touched her in the exact same way, told her the exact same words, "It's your fault. You're bad." Knowing he had listened to his wife's story with apparently no remorse for his own actions, infuriated her. Maggie lost all respect for her dad during that ride.

"You look like hell!" Rose exclaimed when her friend alit from the train. Denise Arlton had called her daughter to tell her about Mrs. Stelson. She wanted Rosie to be prepared when she met Maggie. Rose had not anticipated the degree of Maggie's pain.

Mags was quiet the whole ride back to the dorm. Entering her room, she placed her bags on the floor and stretched out on the bed. Ray left her alone and went back to her studies. For the first time, Rose felt helpless, not knowing what to say or do.

From that day on, Maggie was a changed person. She talked when she had to, begged off when invited out with friends, and withdrew more and more into her own little world. She began to sleep a great deal and rarely ate. It was as if she had fallen into a great abyss and couldn't get out. Maybe she didn't want to get out.

"I'm really worried about her," Rose confided to her psych professor one day after class. Maggie was in the same class, and this was the third consecutive one she had missed. Both her professor and her friend knew this was not typical behavior for Maggie.

Dr. Snipley gave Rose a piece of paper. "This is a note telling Maggie I want to see her in my office. Give it to her when you get back. Let's hope she comes."

After Rose left, 'Skip' Snipley called a colleague, Dr. Dan Edgewood. Dan was the counseling psychologist on campus. Dr. Snipley knew if anyone could help Maggie, he could.

The next day, Margaret Stelson knocked shyly on her professor's door. "Sit down, Maggie." Dr. Snipley was surprised at how gaunt and pale she looked. "I'd like to talk with you."

A half hour later, Skip introduced Maggie to Dr. Edgewood and headed for his next class. He was sure he was leaving her in capable hands.

Margaret JoAnn Stelson found a friend and confidant that day. She felt so relaxed with him, she just talked continuously, as if she were a pent- up river and the dam burst. When the soon-to-be sophomore left the office of this man, she was totally drained, yet feeling light and free as she never had before.

Even though, Maggie said nothing to Rose about the day's events, her roommate knew she was on the road to recovery. Mags continued to see Dan Edgewood every week for the remainder of her college career.

Dr. Roberts, the Deaf Ed. director, hired Maggie to work in the Deaf Studies office during the summer between her freshman and sophomore year.

She was able to stay in the dorm and take a couple of courses at the same time. Maggie was extremely grateful for the encouragement and support from the two Dr. Dans in her life.

Throughout the summer, Maggie began to make many break-throughs with Dr. Edgewood. She looked forward to their weekly talks. Her friends noticed the positive changes in her. Mags was smiling and laughing again, and had regained a lot of her lost energy.

Rose had gone home to help in her dad's shop for the summer so Maggie wrote often and called her every Tuesday with an update on her visits with her "savior", as she blasphemously called Dan.

"Seriously," she said to her dearest friend, "I realize he is only human and actually I am doing the work, but he has, in a real way, saved my life."

"You don't need to explain to me." Rose laughed at Maggie's newly found enthusiasm. "I understand." Each week, she would hang up the phone and thank God for her friends miraculous recovery.

It was October of her junior year that Dan suggested to Maggie that they schedule her appointments for once a month.

"You are making great progress." he assured her, "and now that you've found your 'dream pad' off campus, you won't have the stress of dorm life to contend with. What do you say - do you want to try once a month?"

Outwardly, Maggie agreed. Inside, she wished she could be as sure as he was about her progress. What was it that she was afraid to tell him? There *was* something; she knew it.

When Maggie nodded and said okay Dan smiled broadly. "Good," he said.

Dr. Edgewood, a rugged looking man in his mid thirties, had black shoulder length hair and a nicely trimmed beard with much more gray than was on his head. His green eyes were very much alert and filled with kindness and understanding. He was a great listener who always seemed to know the right thing to say.

He shook Maggie's hand and told her, "I'm proud of you, Maggie. You are one brave girl." However, as he watched her leave he couldn't help thinking there was something there that she wasn't facing. Anyhow, he was meeting Lou 'Skip' Snipley for lunch so couldn't dwell on it just then. He grabbed his windbreaker and headed for the Student Union.

"Mags, that's great! I'm happy for you!" Rose gave her a hug. "God knows you've worked hard. What?" Rose saw doubt surface on Maggie's face.

"I hope I'm ready," Maggie confessed, wishing her confidence was as great as Rose and Dan's. "He says I'm doing great, but I keep thinking there is something I need to tell him. I just don't know what it is. I guess it can't be too important if I can't remember." She just shrugged her shoulders and changed the subject. "Let's go down to Pizza Palace and indulge," she said. The young ladies donned their jackets and headed down Commonwealth Avenue.

"Maggie Stelson is making great strides," Dan said to Skip over lunch. "I can't help thinking, though, that there's something more than what she's telling me. I don't think she's deliberately holding back, however. I don't believe she, herself, knows what it is. There's still some sadness lurking in those lovely brown eyes of hers."

The next two years seemed to fly by for Maggie and Rose. Mags kept busy with classes, working part time for Dan Roberts, attending as many Deaf functions as she could (in order to improve her signing skills), and meeting with Dan Edgewood. Rose ran in opposite directions with her business and philosophy classes. Maggie still couldn't understand her need for philosophy, but Rose did, so that was what mattered. Rose was also one of the editors for the school paper and on the yearbook committee. The pair shared an apartment, but communicated ninety percent of the time by writing notes.

Finally it was the last semester of their senior year. As exam time drew near, Rose practically glued herself to the one desk in their apartment while Maggie spent her days in the library either researching or at the computer. Rose had two written and two oral exams. Maggie had two projects and a research paper all due on the final day of exams. She quizzed Rose on the great philosophers of the nineteenth and twentieth centuries. Rose listened to her arguments for teaching language to Deaf children, the difference between language and speech, and knew the theories behind bilingual/bi-cultural education almost as well as her friend. The two chums encouraged and rooted for each other constantly.

"We make a great team, don't we?" Ray commented. The girls were taking a well-deserved break from their studies.

"Yeah," Mags responded. "Mrs. Frazier doesn't know what she created making me ambassador back in third grade."

Rose was the first one up the next day. Soon she was joined at the table by Maggie, awakened by the smell of freshly brewed coffee.

"Well, May twelfth arrives at last. I am so nervous about my exam. My philosophy prof is tough. He's a stickler for details. I hope I do okay. More importantly, I hope I don't throw up in the middle of it."

Maggie laughed and laughed. "You'll do fine as always. Cripe, you know the stuff inside out and backwards. To quote what a good friend always says to me, 'Don't be such a worry wart.' "

Rose guffawed as she headed for the shower.

Rose left for her exam at seven thirty. The girls agreed to meet at the Union to celebrate, after Maggie delivered her paper at noon. Maggie never made it to the rendezvous.

Arriving home after three, Maggie heard "Where the hell have you been?" Unable to answer, she stood in the doorway and cried out of pure joy.

Ray's softer question brought her back to the moment. "Okay, who is he?"

Maggie babbled like a young teenager having her first crush. "Oh, Ray, I just met the man I intend to marry. He is absolutely wonderful. I was walking back to meet you and I tripped on a tree root. Suddenly I looked up and there he was. I thought I was seeing things, like I hit my head or something. Then he helped me up and as usual I stuck my foot in my mouth, rambling on. But you know what? He's Deaf! He just pointed to his ears, smiled, and began to walk away. I almost let him go before I came out of my daze. Catching up to him, I began to sign, and he grinned. I thanked him and asked him to have lunch with me."

Claire M. Ford

"*You* asked *him?*" Rose interrupted her friend. "You *never* do things like that. Maybe you did bump your head," she teased. "I just can't believe you did that, Maggie. He must be special." Rose said incredulously.

"Shut up and let me finish," Maggie laughed. "He took me to a little restaurant in Harvard Square, owned by his brother, who is also Deaf. The food was wonderful and we just talked. He told me all about himself and I felt so comfortable and relaxed with him.

"Rose, he is twenty four and finishing up his master's in school administration. His dream is to run his own school someday. Oh, by the way, his name is Jeffery Reyfield and he's from Beverly. It's about twenty miles north of here. He commutes to classes and lives at home. He has two brothers and one sister. Dave, who owns the restaurant, and their parents are also Deaf. His dad retired last year, and works part-time doing maintenance work at the Beverly School for the Deaf, where Dave and Jeff went to school. Jeff works with his dad summers and weekends.

"Rose, I think I love him. He said he'd call me again and I sure hope he does. I hate the thought of graduating and going back to New York. What am I going to do? I've never felt this way before." Maggie sat back in the chair with a loud sigh.

Excited for her long-time chum, Rose suggested they somehow celebrate Mags' good fortune.

"Tonight," she lectured, "You just need to feel the happiness and relish your amazing luck. Tomorrow we can figure out how to keep you near- by. So, get your purse and let's go get a banana split or some other purely fattening thing."

"Oh, no, I can't!" Maggie moaned. "What if I go out and he calls? I have to stay home."

Rose got up and stood in front of her roommate. "You are crazy, you know that? And I am *extremely* jealous. This one time, I will walk to the Ice Cream Company, and bring back treats. You sit by the TTY and wait. Maybe if you stare hard enough, the phone will ring."

182

"Ha, ha, ha," retorted Maggie. But when Rose left, she did just that. Maggie was extremely glad that she had convinced her parents to buy her a TTY for Christmas last year.

"Mom, Dad, it is a telephone device used by Deaf people so they can talk on the phone. To talk you simply place the receiver in the cups provided and type your message. It's only fair if you work with Deaf people to have one, otherwise you have to go through a third person and that is awful. You have no privacy. Guys, since my advisor is Deaf, I will use it. That is all I want for Christmas."

Maggie found the machine invaluable and was glad to be able to tell Jeff she had one. Now if only he'd call.

It was two days, two long, frantic days, before Jeff finally called Maggie. Rose picked up the phone and said hello. Placing the receiver on the table, she walked over and knocked on the bathroom door. "Mags, I think it's for you. All I hear is beep-beep."

She bolted back when the door flew open, and Maggie ran out in her underwear with her wet hair stuck to her head. "Hello," she typed. When she hung up, Maggie was a new woman. Jeff had finally called.

The day before graduation, Dan Roberts called Maggie into his office and explained that she was being offered a scholarship to continue her studies for her Master's degree.

"The Massachusetts Association of the Deaf offers one a year, and you have the highest grades of all eleven students in the Deaf Studies department. If you wish to receive it, I'll award it to you at graduation tomorrow night."

"*If I wish?*" Maggie screamed with delight. "It's like a dream come true. Of course I want it!"

"It only covers tuition, so if you want to keep your job as my secretary, it's yours," he added.

Rose was so excited for her chum. She had decided to go for her CPA degree at the University of New York in Buffalo so she could work with her dad at the same time.

Claire M. Ford

"It'll take longer to go part-time," she said, "but I believe it is for the best."

"Tina Winslow asked me if you'd think about her for a new roommate. She'll be continuing her studies as well." Tina was a mutual friend whom they grew close to while living in the dorm. Tina spent many a night studying with them when things got too rowdy around her.

"I'll call her right away," Maggie exclaimed. Then in a more somber voice, she confided "I'll miss you, Rose but I know we'll keep in touch."

"You bet," Rose said tearfully. "It won't be that long before we're together again. Besides, there's always the phone. And," she added emphatically, " Don't forget me when you plan your wedding."

The pair just laughed while Maggie called Tina.

Finally, graduation night came and went. The two brand new alumni members hugged as Rose got ready to head north with her parents. Maggie's folks kissed her goodbye and wished her luck.

"We're very proud of you, princess." Her dad gave her a hug. She pulled away quickly and couldn't understand why she was so uncomfortable.

"Be sure to call and tell us when you plan to come in July. And bring Jeff. He'll be very welcome," her mom whispered into her ear as she hugged her daughter. "Be good."

Maggie stood arm in arm with Jeff as she waved goodbye.

Maggie took two courses that summer, worked as many hours as she could in the Deaf Studies office, met with Dan E. twice, and saw Jeff almost every night. Needless to say, she was extremely busy and happy.

It was only when she left Dan's office that a feeling of melancholy hit her.

I know there's something more, she thought. *I just wish I could remember.*

184

He had suggested there was nothing more he could do, so it may be a good time to terminate their sessions. This scared Maggie to death. "But why?" she groaned.

She had to put it out of her head for now, because she and Jeff were heading for Buffalo that afternoon.

Chapter Twenty-Three

It was in Buffalo that Maggie began to remember what she had been blocking for so long.

Molly met the young couple at the train station. Maggie couldn't help commenting on how well she looked.

"I'm doing everything the doctor has told me to," her mother responded proudly. "Eat right, sleep right, exercise. "I feel better than I have in a long time."

Maggie interpreted for Jeff all the way home. Upon arrival, he grinned when Molly signed for herself, "Welcome to our home."

Rose came over that evening and the three young people went out to eat and went bowling. Ray learned quite a bit of sign that night and intended to learn more.

Two nights later, Molly had pulled out all the old photo albums for Maggie to share with Jeff. The two of them sat side by side on the couch pointing out pictures that brought to mind some of the crazy antics she had done as a child.

"Here's one of me when I was learning how to feed myself." They laughed together, wondering where her face was under all the oatmeal.

They found one of her and her Panda. She and Jake sitting in the big lounge chair together. She and mom curled up side by side in mom's bed. One of her in her pretty yellow nightie with Sophie brushing her clean hair. Maggie suddenly grew very quiet and her eyes filled with tears. Not hearing any laughter, Jake and Molly poked their heads in from the kitchen. Just at that same moment,

Maggie took the photo album and threw it hard against the opposite wall.

Not knowing what to do, Jeff went over and started picking up the pictures while Maggie put her head in her hands and sobbed. Jake looked at Molly, then went to try and comfort his daughter. When he placed his hand on her shoulder, all the rage she had pent up inside of her came out.

She screamed at the man who supposedly loved her: "Don't you touch me. Don't you ever touch me again! I hate you!"

"Maggie, princess -" he began, but got no further.

"Don't call me that. You thought I'd forget, didn't you? You hoped I would never say anything. So you made me believe I was bad. It was my fault. Well, I *do* remember! Now I know what's been bothering me for so long."

Her tears streamed and her voice shook, but she continued.

"You abused me a lot when I was little. You would touch me and make me touch you. You told me it was a secret, special love between father and daughter. I hated it. It hurt and I hated it. But you were my daddy and I believed you. I was so confused. I wondered how a father could love his little girl and hurt her at the same time."

"Mom," Maggie hissed through clenched teeth, never taking her eyes of her father's pale face, "Mom, this man that you love so much, your husband, my father, raped me just like Uncle Phil did to you. I remember it was the night of my sixth birthday. My father raped his six-year-old daughter!"

Maggie was near hysterics, but she went on. It was if a dam had burst and she couldn't stop the flow of words. "Many nights he would come into my room and pull up my nightie, touching my genitals and rubbing my bottom. Sometimes he would stick his finger in my rectum or vagina. Sometimes he made me touch him or kiss his penis. But when I was six, he fondled me all over and stuck his penis inside me, and I cried it hurt so bad. When he finished and left, I wet the bed and wished I would die.

"He did it a few more times, but that was the worst. That was the worst night of my entire life. He raped me, he abused me, he treated me like shit! And, and-"

Maggie sat and sobbed as if her heart would break. Jeff and Molly stood there dumbfounded. Jeff had no idea what she was saying but saw the anguish of her words. He went and put his arms around his girlfriend.

Molly couldn't move. It was as if she was glued to the spot. She just stared at her husband questioningly. No words would come.

Jake moved to his wife and taking her arm, walked her back in to the kitchen.

"Mol, believe me, it's not true. She saw a picture of you and Phil and projected your problems on to herself. It must be the stress of all she's been through. Molly, you have to believe me - I never did all those things," Jake was pleading with her now.

As her shock wore off, Molly began to respond. "I don't know what to believe. I can't imagine you doing that, especially when you were so shocked that it had happened to me. Right now I have to get help for Maggie. I'm going to call Linda."

After spending two hours with the girl, Linda was convinced she was not making it up. Before dismissing Maggie, she called Dr. Edgewood in Boston, with Maggie's permission, of course. He explained his feeling that she was holding something back and felt this was real. He offered to come up the following day and Linda was grateful.

An interpreter from Deaf School had come over to explain things to Jeff, and he cried for the woman he loved. Linda went to talk to the Stelsons and suggested that Maggie spend a few days in the hospital. They agreed, and went to say good night to her. Maggie would not speak and just kept staring straight ahead. Molly knew those symptoms all too well.

"Jake," Molly urged, "please swear to me you didn't do what she said."

"Mol, I swear with all my being. I did not." Somehow, he would convince her that Maggie was crazy. He had to.

189

Jeff stayed at the school for the Deaf and visited Maggie each day. He believed her, and hated her father for what he did to her. Molly would come in after work and sit with Maggie. Maggie would not talk to her. Rose was there as much as she could, and couldn't believe what Maggie had been through as a little girl. Her heart ached for her friend, and she could no longer look Mr. Stelson in the eye.

Maggie was released on the fourth day, and she and Jeff headed back to Boston. Since Tina was in Hawaii with her folks for two weeks, Rose went to stay with her long time soul mate. Maggie slept a great deal and met with Dan daily. She remembered more and more details and would come home from each session looking ghastly. Jeff came over every evening and spent time with her. He grew deeply in love with her.

He was finishing up his Master's thesis and Dan Roberts had a great career idea for him.

In fact, they were going to approach the president of the college next week with their plans.

Maggie had decided to postpone working for her Master's. Maybe she'd pick it up again, but right now she only wanted to get well.

Finally, in October, Jeff asked Maggie to marry him.

"I know we have only known each other since May but I love you and want to marry you. Please say you love me, too. Say you will marry me."

Maggie signed back without hesitation. "I do love you and I will marry you."

Jeff kissed her and placed a ring on her finger. Dave had helped him pay for it and coached him on the proposing part. He would have to call Dave right away and tell him it had worked. They ran upstairs, to tell Rose, who was ecstatic.

"Of course, you'll be my maid of honor," Maggie stated emphatically. Turning to Jeff, she asked, "Can we get married on February 27? I know it's only four and a half months but it's a special date for me.

"You never told me that," Rose said. "Why is it so special?"

"I was too embarrassed." Maggie blushed. "You two will probably think I'm nuts, but when I was little I lived in a dream world wishing someone would love me. Then, on February 27, 1975 when I was six and a half I had the mumps. Dad bought me the movie of Snow White. I had seen it many times before, but this time the movie was *mine*. When I watched it and the prince took her away, I believed he was my prince taking me away from all the hurt. Now my dream has come true and my real prince is here. I *will* live happily ever after." She just smiled and her two friends did likewise.

Maggie went home for Thanksgiving, alone, to tell her mother about her engagement. She no longer spoke to or about her dad. However, for her mother's sake she would be civil. She knew her mom believed her father over her. She also knew the truth would come out someday, and prayed her mother would survive it.

"The date is February 27 and it will be held at St. John Church in Beverly. That's where Jeff and his family attend and they're able to provide interpreters and so on. They're used to dealing with Deaf people," Maggie stopped abruptly when Jake entered the room.

"Congratulations, princess." He tried to sound less nervous than he felt. "I'm very proud of you. We'd both love to come, wouldn't we, Mol?"

Maggie took a deep breath and spoke with remarkable calm. "Dad, I do not want you at my wedding. You have hurt me too much in my lifetime, and I can't let the pain go if I see you. After tonight you will never see me again. Mom is always welcome in my house, but you are not. I don't know how you made Mom believe your lies, but we both know the truth, don't we, Dad? If you fight me on this, or show up at my wedding, I'll press charges against you."

Turning to her mom, she continued "I'm sorry, Mom, but I'll not deny what happened, even if he does. I'm sorry you can't believe me, but I understand. I love you, Mom."

Maggie left Buffalo the following day, never intending to return. She had learned that Pat and Sophie had moved out to California to try and escape the New York winters. Pat had asked

Molly to run the shop in Buffalo until she could find a buyer. For a few months the two women toured the state, taking note of such things as climate, scenery, and business opportunities. They had finally settled in sunny Palm Springs. There, they opened a new shop which they called, "The Oasis". It was an instant delight and already they were showing a profit. Mags would send an invitation to them in California.

Maggie hadn't heard from her parents at all since she left after Thanksgiving. She and Jeff spent the Christmas holidays in Beverly with his family. Rose called them saying she had met a wonderful man named Kevin and had been seeing him for a little over two weeks. She hoped they were having a great Christmas and Santa was good to them.

"Also," she said excitedly, "Dad said he could do without me for the next two months, so I can come help you plan for your wedding."

Maggie kept so busy that she lost complete track of the days. Pat wrote that she and Sophie planned to come at the end of January. Her gift to Mags and Jeff was to cater the complete affair without charge. "I will not take no for an answer," Pat stated emphatically. "So get used to the idea."

When Maggie told Jeff, he laughed hysterically. "I guess we'd better let her," he signed. Mags threw her arms around him and kissed him long and hard. He looked at her and signed, "FOR-FOR", which in English means what did you do that for? She just shrugged and said, "Because I'm so very happy."

On January 22 there was a knock on the apartment door. It was ten in the morning and snowing outside. Maggie and Rose were sitting having coffee and planning the church service. Startled, they looked at each other, wondering who was knocking. Maggie was surprised to open the door and see Linda Terrio standing there.

She introduced Linda to Rose, offered her a seat and brought her a cup of coffee. When she sat down again, Maggie realized how tense she was.

"Maggie." Linda spoke softly and slowly." I'm sorry to have to tell you this, but your father killed himself yesterday. Since Thanksgiving, he and Molly have been separated. He couldn't convince her to come back. I really believe he loved her and you." Linda saw the hatred on Maggie's face and went on.

"Jake left a note on the table which read:

Molly, I never meant to hurt you or Maggie. I was so lonely and empty feeling. Please forgive me and ask Maggie to do the same. I did hurt her as she said.

It was wrong and I'm so sorry. I have lived with the pain and guilt of my actions all my life. I can't live with them any more.

I love you, both.

J.

He then hanged himself on one of the old pipes in the cellar."

"Mom where's mom?" Maggie was as white as a sheet.

"Your mother is back in Rochester. She has had a major setback, and right now is on sedatives and a strong antidepressant. She asked me to tell you that she loves you and wishes you the best for you wedding. I'm afraid she won't be able to get there."

Maggie was about to throw up and ran to the bathroom. Rose started to follow but Linda held her back.

"Give her the time alone," Linda chided softly. "I know this is a hard time for this to happen. Let's just hope and pray she'll be able to handle it."

Maggie came out of the bathroom looking like she was about to faint. Linda and Rose ran to help her to the couch.

"I have to put off the wedding," she stuttered. "No, I can't, it's too late!" Oh, what am I going to do?" Maggie cried as if her heart would break. "It's all my fault," she repeated. "It's all my fault."

Claire M. Ford

At Linda's suggestion, Rose brought Mags two aspirin and a glass of water. After her friend took the pills and laid back on the sofa, Rose gently wiped her face with a warm face cloth. Thankfully, it didn't take long for the young woman to fall asleep.

Linda filled Rose in on the funeral arrangements and offered to stay in town to accompany the girls to the funeral. At Rose's insistence, she stayed over at the apartment. The following morning the trio left for New York in Linda's little Pinto.

Maggie attended the services for her father with Jeff and the Arltons. She sat through it as if in a trance. Her face remained stoic and she never shed a tear. Her mom was unable to be there, of course. The group left the cemetery immediately, as Maggie didn't want to talk to anyone. She slept all that afternoon and when she awoke it was as if nothing ever happened. Maggie bounced downstairs, talking about getting back to her wedding plans.

On their way out of town the following morning, Rose, Jeff and Maggie stopped briefly to visit Molly.

"It's me, Mom, Maggie," she touched the arm of the sleeping woman. Linda had warned them that Molly had been heavily sedated so they weren't shocked when they saw her. Molly never even knew that she, Jeff and Rose were there that day.

"Hi, Mom. It's me." Back at the apartment, Mags went to take a long bath so Rose took the opportunity to call home. "I wanted to let you know that Maggie's going to be okay. She sobbed on Jeff's shoulder much of the way home. She talked about her dad and what he did to her and her mom. My heart ached to listen to her. I couldn't believe how he had abused her. By the time we got here, she seemed more relaxed and calmer. God, mom she has been through so much in her lifetime. I just can't imagine how she survived. I'm so glad she found Jeff. He loves her so much and I know he'll make her happy."

Ray said goodbye and hung up quickly when she heard the bathroom door open.

Maggie fell into a deep sleep the minute she hit the pillow and didn't stir till morning.

Chapter Twenty-Four

Margaret JoAnn Stelson arose to a beautiful sunny day. There was snow left over from a storm the week before but not enough to hinder her guests from getting to the wedding. Rose was asleep beside her in the large queen-sized brass bed. Feeling mischievous, Maggie blew in her friend's ear like she used to a long time before. Ray jumped with a start and opened her eyes to see Maggie doubled over with laughter.

Donned in robes and slippers, the pair trooped downstairs to the kitchen in hopes of discovering some coffee. Arriving at the door, they smiled at each other simultaneously. Both had recognized the freshly brewed aroma.

The young women were staying at Jeff's house in North Beverly until the wedding. Since it was bad luck for the groom to see the bride, Jeff had been exiled to his older brother's house in Cambridge. Dave would bring him right to the church. The ceremony was scheduled for three in the afternoon.

Mrs. Harriet Reyfield was sitting at the kitchen table when Maggie and Rose arrived. Mags tapped her on the shoulder and signed "good morning".

"Good morning to you, too," she signed. "Would you girls like some coffee?"

Both girls nodded and Harriet ordered them to sit. A moment later, she was back with two steaming mugs which she placed in front of them. Leaving them again, she soon returned with huge blueberry and bran muffins.

"Eddie picked these up at The Donut Hole this morning. There are more for your guests when they arrive."

Maggie didn't think she could eat, but Harriet insisted. "You don't want to faint from hunger. You must eat, trust me."

The bride-to-be tried one bite, smiled, and devoured the monster of a pastry.

Rose and Harriet just looked at each other and giggled.

At 1:00 PM, Rose's two sisters arrived, as did Anna Reyfield. They were to be bridesmaids for the ceremony. No one had to even ask who the Maid of Honor would be: Rose, of course.

The young women giggled and chattered as they helped Maggie make the transformation from petrified lady-in-waiting, to the most beautiful bride imaginable. Looking in the mirror while Rose reached up and placed her veil in place, Maggie could not believe this was happening to her. Never before in her life had she felt so beautiful or so happy.

Iris, Lily and Anna gasped when they saw her.

"You look radiant," Anna whispered in her ear. "My little brother is the luckiest man in the world. Next to my husband, of course." Anna turned up her nose in mock snobbery and walked away as the other four playfully booed and hissed.

Iris and Lily also hugged and kissed her, praising her looks. They left the room to head for the car, leaving Rose and Margaret alone in the room.

"Well, Miss Ambassador, this is it. How do you feel?" Rose Arlton was so proud she could burst. "I can't believe my best friend in the whole world is about to wed. I'm so happy for you, Mags."

She gave her friend a great big hug. "I love you so much, friend."

"Ray, I'm so nervous," Maggie confided in her chum. "What if I trip or something?" Then a little more seriously, she said soberly, "Do you think I'm doing the right thing? I don't want Jeff and I to end up like my folks. I want a storybook wedding and 'happily-ever-after' marriage. Am I being naive?"

"Mags, you are one hell of a person. Jeff loves you so much and you love him. You have nothing to worry about. Just remember" -

Rose suddenly got motherly again. - "marriages are not free of problems and hardships. I believe communication is the key. Watching my parents, they could always tell each other how they felt, and always told each other 'I love you'. Just be open-minded and listen to each other, and you'll have a great marriage. Listen to your marriage counselor and obey. You hear me?" The girls laughed and hugged again, then headed to the limo.

Jeff had been pacing the sanctuary of the church for half an hour. He continuously looked at his watch while wearing a hole in the rug. Dave teased him to relax or he'd be too tired for the honeymoon.

"Do you have the ring?" Jeff signed. "Is the interpreter ready? What if she changes her mind?"

Finally Dave grabbed his brother by the shoulders and held him still. "Stay," he signed. When he had his younger brother's attention, he continued. "Maggie loves you; she will not change her mind. Everything'll be okay - you'll see. Once you catch Maggie's eye as she walks down the aisle, you'll forget there's anyone else in the church. Take it from one who knows."

Dave had married his high school sweetheart when he was twenty-five. He and Rita had two daughters ages four and two, and a third child on the way. His speech helped Jeff to relax a bit.

No sooner had he calmed down then Jeff felt a tap on his shoulder. He jumped three feet in the air and turned to face the priest, Father Everard.

"It's time to start," he explained through the interpreter and Jeff's face went pale with anxiety.

The groom walked as close to Dave, his best man, as he could, so as not to fall. When they reached their place at the front of the church, Jeff turned to see the crowd seated in the pews. The ushers at the back of the church were awaiting the female members of the wedding party. Jeff spotted his parents in the second row and smiled when his dad gave him the "thumb's up" sign. Beside his folks were Jenny and Katie, Dave's little girls who simply adored their Uncle Jeff.

The wedding march began and everyone stood. Then Jeff knew exactly what his brother meant.

As he spotted Maggie walking on the arm of Fred Arlton, he beamed a wide grin, and nothing else in the world mattered.

Maggie sat up and stretched as Jeff maneuvered the car into the small parking lot of the well-lit Debbie's Diner. She couldn't believe she could be hungry with all the food Auntie Pat had provided for her reception, yet she felt famished.

The couple found a booth just being cleaned and slid into the pale yellow seats. Both ordered the turkey club sandwich with fries and coffee. Mags was annoyed with the waitress who spoke only to her and totally ignored her husband.

"What does he want?" she asked Maggie. She wanted to be sarcastic and tell the waitress to ask him herself, but Jeff caught her eye and said no.

"But she was so rude!" Maggie signed with stress. "You don't deserve that!"

"I know," her groom signed calmly. "But let it go this time. I don't want it to spoil our day. Darling, you looked so beautiful. I love you so much."

Maggie relaxed in her seat and grinned. "You always know just what to say." She leaned over the table and kissed him tenderly. Neither heard the cheers from the counter behind them.

As they ate, they reminisced. Neither could remember a great deal about the reception and were glad they had it on video tape. Mags remembered the dancing and how she stepped on his dad's foot, almost causing them to fall. Jeff's happiest recollection was cutting the cake his brother had made for them.

It was during dessert that the new Mrs.

Reyfield felt the guilt and sadness return. She could picture vividly the empty seats where her mother and father should have been. When Jeff mentioned the change in her countenance, she reiterated her wish that they could have been there.

"Maybe if I hadn't said anything," she began again. "Maybe if.."

He stopped her hands in mid-sentence. "Don't do this to your-self. It's not your fault. Please, Maggie - let it go. There's nothing you can do to change it. Don't let it spoil your happiness, darling." His eyes met hers and she saw his anxiety. Her smile and nod told him she was okay again. He slumped back in relief.

The newlyweds finished eating and paid their bill. Soon they were back on the road heading for the Big Apple. They would stay in Greenwich and drive on to Buffalo the following morning. There they would visit with Molly then head on up to Niagara Falls for a two-week stay.

Mags asked Jeff if he wanted her to drive for a while, but he felt he could make it to the hotel. She relaxed in her seat and closed her eyes. It was almost midnight and they didn't expect to reach their hotel for another hour or so.

Sure enough, 1:15 AM was flashing on the neon sign as the cou-ple pulled up to the Greenwich Inn for the night. The pair checked in, and Maggie giggled as Jeff insisted on carrying her over the threshold of room 117.

Chapter Twenty-Five

Gently Maggie closed the door of the nursery. Her daughter, Patricia Jamie Reyfield, was now almost fifteen months old. The baby had been fighting a cold and was quite fussy. Maggie was relieved when she finally settled down to sleep, and didn't want to make any unnecessary noise to waken her.

Maggie tiptoed into the living room, where her adoring husband sat watching an old movie. She gently put her arms around him, and when he looked up, kissed him on the forehead.

Holding her hand, he waltzed his soul mate around the couch where she sat facing him.

"Jeff, I have an idea that I want to share with you," she signed. "Please let me finish before you comment."

Her hands flew for the next ten minutes as her excitement grew with each sentence. When she finished she cautiously asked him, 'What do you think?'

Relief flooded through her as he signed, " I think it's a wonderful idea."

"I know you're very busy at the school, but I feel I need to go tomorrow or the next day at the latest. Do you think maybe Dave and Rita could take Tricia?"

Jeff's mom had passed away only three months after their wedding, and his dad now lived with his sister in Illinois. Dave, his wife Rita and their three daughters lived in Newton.

"Dave's probably at the restaurant, but I'll call Rita and ask her about it. I can take tomorrow off and drive you to the train, then bring Trish to Newton." Jeff loved Maggie so much he would do anything to make her happy.

He went in to the den to make the call.

"You watch the movie and tell me what I miss."

Mags laid her head back against the couch and grinned like a Cheshire cat.

God, I love that man, she thought to herself.

He came in a short time later to tell her it was all arranged.

"Rita said they'd be thrilled to watch her. But be prepared; Her girls will probably spoil our daughter rotten. I told her Trish was fighting a cold. She laughed and said not to worry she was experienced. Now you go pack and do whatever you need to do. Then we can relax together."

"I'm all ready," she responded slyly. " I hope you don't get mad, but I called Mike Stephenson, at his office. I asked him if that house in Hingham was still available. He said it was, and I told him you'd most likely be by tomorrow to bid on it."

Jeff just laughed and pulled his lovely wife into his lap. "I knew you were up to something when you asked all those questions last week."

After their honeymoon, Jeff and Maggie had returned to Boston so that Jeff could bring closure to some deal he and Dan Roberts had been working on. He kept Maggie in suspense because he refused to tell her until it was finalized.

"Come on," she'd tease. "I won't tell anyone. You can trust me."

Every time she tried this tactic, he would purse his lips, try to look annoyed and tell her no. He'd walk away with a twinkle in his eye and she would pretend to be infuriated with him. However, she knew he'd tell her when he was ready.

June first was the day of decision. Jeff was a wreck, but a handsome wreck, when he left their rented apartment to meet Dan Roberts for their 1:30 meeting. The two of them were meeting with the president of Boston University, Ronald Fredrickson, as well as the superintendent of schools and president of the school board from Randolph , Dean of Education, and the board of trustees of the local School for the Deaf.

Coming in to the kitchen, Jeff tapped Maggie on the shoulder. "Do I look okay?" he asked. Jeff stood before her in his navy blue suit, which he had her iron for him the night before. With it, he had on a light blue shirt and the tie she had given him for his birthday. It had very narrow, slanted lines, alternating colors blue, green and yellow, and it matched the suit perfectly. His hair was combed to perfection and he even trimmed his beard, a ritual he performed only once a week. His shoes were polished until they shone.

Maggie signed, "You look wonderful, extremely handsome. Jefferey Reyfield - you're a looker." Of course, she had to explain the idiom to her Deaf mate. She added, "If I didn't know your meeting was important, I would throw myself at your feet and beg you to make love to me. You look so sexy."

He just laughed and gave his wife a long sensual kiss and waved as he walked out the door.

Three hours later, he was back with contract in hand, ready to celebrate. He picked Maggie up off the floor and spun her around the room. When the two were dizzy with joy and excitement, he sat her down on the couch and told her the news.

"The School for the Deaf has been in danger of closing," he began. "The committee who run it are considering pulling out and leaving it to the city and state to run. The problem is the city can't afford it since the student population is so low and the costs so high. So Dan and I came up with a great plan, which I developed as my Master's thesis, and the city representative and superintendent as well as everyone else at the meeting accepted our proposal."

Maggie didn't understand all of what he told her, but got the general idea.

He and Dan convinced the faculty of Boston University to invest in the Deaf School for a five year term. It would become a satellite school of BU, so to speak. BU would select an administrator to run the school for the five years, to build up the school and get it on its feet again. The administrator would hire the staff needed to make it a volatile investment.

At the end of five years, the thriving school would become city-and-state-funded, or sold if it didn't work out. Jeff presented his research showing how the goal could be accomplished. He brought in everything from curriculum, to dorms logistics, to public relations.

By the end of the meeting, Jeff had them sold on the idea.

"Not only did they like my ideas," he signed enthusiastically, "They appointed me administrator for the five-year term, with a promise of tenure if my ideas pay off."

It was a chance of a lifetime for Jeff, and Mags was so proud of her husband. Ever since she met him this was the dream he talked about. She was ecstatic over the news and agreed to a celebration.

"Mr. Jeffery Reyfield, I am so proud of you. I will be honored to accompany an important person such as yourself to the finest restaurant in town. But before I go change, I want to tell you my news." She looked into his face with a sheepish grin and paused for effect. Finally she announced. "Mr. Reyfield, I, your wife, am pregnant."

It took a minute for the words to register, but Maggie knew just when they did. Jeff's face went from serious, to glowing, to worry, to questioning in about five seconds.

That night the two went dining and dancing until early morning and when they arrived home they made love to each other until dawn. They were asleep in each other's arms when the phone rang.

Drowsily, Maggie reached over to answer it, and was surprised to hear her mother's voice on the line. Molly was home and feeling better. She went back to Rochester periodically, as the house was just too lonely for her, and held too many memories. However, Maggie's mom had seemed to be handling things pretty well as of late.

When Maggie hung up, Jeff pulled her near him. "Is anything wrong?"

"No, Mom just wanted to say hello. I asked her why she called so early and do you know it's almost noon? Anyhow, she wanted to know how you were, and what I wanted for my birthday, and so on. I told her we had a late night and were just now waking up and asked if I could call her back later. I want to tell her about the baby."

Maggie sauntered in to take a shower. Then when her beloved went to take his, she trotted down to the kitchen to fix breakfast - or brunch, actually.

January 3, 1995, Patricia Jamie Reyfield came into the world. The Arltons sent a beautiful bouquet of pink carnations laced with baby's breath, and a gorgeous plant arrived from Pat and Sophie.

The next morning, Mags heard a knock at the door of her private room and screamed with delight when Rose and Kevin walked in. Rose had married Kevin the past September, and insisted Maggie stand up with her, even though she was six months pregnant. The newlyweds were destined to become godparents to the beautiful baby girl Rose was now holding.

Trish, as they intended to call her, weighed in at 6.5 pounds. She had curly hair, a shade lighter than Maggie's, and Jeff's pretty blue eyes.

Molly had also come down from New York and squealed when she entered the room. She immediately ran to give Rose a bear hug and then Kevin.

"You look great," Rose told her sincerely.

Molly had been doing much better. Though she still depended on her visits to the clinic, they were much less frequent, and her bouts with depression were now short-lived. Physically, she had put on some of the weight she lost, and began exercising again. She had a cold early in November which had to be watched carefully. The doctors were relieved when she was able to fight it off. Molly was doing very well. She stayed two weeks with Jeff and Maggie.

Throughout the year, Maggie kept in contact with Molly and sent her many pictures of the baby. She tried to get to Buffalo as often as she could, knowing how lonely her mother was.

Jeff was very busy with school and his plans were proving insightful and workable. Sometimes Mags scolded him about working too hard, but she was so proud of him. He was very happy and content. He adored his daughter. Daddy insisted it would be his job to bathe Trish and put her to bed. Maggie was nervous at first, then reprimanded herself for judging him by her father's standards.

Shut up Maggie, she'd tell herself. *He would never hurt his daughter that way!*

That year the Reyfield's were looking for a house along with everything else. The townhouse they were renting was small and was located on a very busy street. They wanted a place with extra room for more children, as well as a large yard for Trish to play in.

The realtor had shown them a few houses in Hingham in the past few weeks. One of them was a duplex, which he said could be an ideal investment. They could knock down a few walls and make it in to a one family, or if they chose, they could rent out one side. One side had three bedrooms, the other two.

Maggie had liked it because of the high ceilings, spacious sunny rooms, and a screened-in porch overlooking a large back yard. "They are good qualities," Jeff agreed on the ride home. "But what do we need a duplex for? I think if we find a one family home with the same qualities, it would save money, not to mention time and work."

For the next two days, Maggie did a great deal of thinking, questioning, and planning. Once her plan was formulated she presented it to Jeff, and now she sat wrapped in his arms filled with relief and an ever-deepening love for her husband.

It was April 5th when Maggie surprised her mom by arriving on her doorstep. She stayed for a week, sharing her idea with Molly, who loved it immediately. The two talked, laughed, cried, and consoled each other for the next seven days. When Maggie was riding home, she went over everything in her head to make sure every detail was taken care of.

206

On April 7th, Jeff called her to say he put a bid in on the house and it had been accepted.

"The workers can start tomorrow and promised to have the job done by June 1. Tom, the owners' realtor, agreed that the day could also be the day we pass papers and close the deal."

Mags relayed the message to her mom who applauded with joy. The next day she and Maggie met with a realtor in town to place Molly's house on the market.

"Yes," Maggie sighed, "It'll work. I know it will." She leaned back and fell asleep.

Chapter Twenty-Six

True to her word, Maggie boarded the train June 2nd, the day after the papers were signed, and headed for Rochester. She arrived at her destination at 2:00 PM and immediately headed to the information booth to her left.

"There's a Johnson's rental place on the next block", the gentleman told her. Smiling. she thanked him for the information, pushed her way through the crowds, and went out the door.

The man was right. Just up the street was the rental place. Maggie could see the sign as soon as she emerged from the station. The clerk was not at all what she expected. He was short and pudgy, just like the cigar he was chewing on.

The man's attitude seemed to fit him well.

"Lady, you wanna rent a truck? Ladies don't drive trucks. How about a nice, pretty sedan?"

Maggie was tired, hurried, and did not appreciate his condescending remark.

"Look, for your information, ladies can, and do drive trucks as well as any man. I'm not asking for an eighteen-wheeler. All I want is a regular-sized pick-up truck with automatic transmission. If you don't have one available, just tell me and I'll take my business elsewhere. Now, do you want my money or not?"

"Okay, lady, you got it. Just sign these papers. I need some identification and a credit card number."

That young lady has a lot of spunk, he remarked to himself. He smiled as he grabbed the key from the peg board behind him. By the time he returned his attention to her, she had completed the forms.

Maggie handed him the forms and after making arrangements as to where to leave the car in Massachusetts, she took the key from him.

"The truck's out back." He thrust his thumb over his shoulder to indicate where. "The door's over there. It's parked in number fifteen. Pleasant travelin'."

"Thanks," she replied and headed for the back door.

Space number fifteen was easy to find, and she smiled as she opened the vehicle door. He had given her a bright red, wide bed pick-up that looked to be brand new.

Soon Maggie was up in the cab and on her way. The ride to the clinic was fifteen minutes long, but it seemed endless to her. Pulling up to the front door, Maggie spotted her mother waiting for her in the lobby. Mags experienced an exhilaration she hadn't felt in a long time as she pushed open the glass door and entered, walking toward her Mom.

"Mom, you look radiant." She hugged her mother like never before. Molly was sparkling clean and wearing make-up. Her hair had been done quite recently and the style was perfect for her. She was wearing a beautiful powder-blue dress, with white collar and belt. A pearl necklace with matching earrings completed the outfit magnificently.

"Linda took me shopping and to the beautician yesterday." Molly was beaming. "Do I pass inspection?"

"You are absolutely stunning," her daughter remarked. Turning to Linda, who had stayed quietly in the background, Maggie thanked her profusely. "How can I ever thank you enough for all you've done? I hope we can keep in touch, and if you ever get to Massachusetts, you are always welcome." She gave her mom's shrink a grateful hug.

"Your mother is a wonderful woman." Linda smiled at Molly, who was blushing. "She has been through a lot and survived. I'm very proud of her.

"Molly, you have my number. Call me anytime and if you need a week's respite, just give us a call. You are more than welcome."

Two years before, Dr. Linda Terrio was chosen unanimously by the board to be the chief administrator at the clinic in Rochester. She had completed her doctorate six months before and the trustees were positive she would do a wonderful job. She was proving them right.

Molly thanked Linda again as she got up into the truck with her daughter. Her few things which had been boxed and packed earlier had been placed in the bed of the pick-up. Maggie took a minute to squeeze her mother's hand and kiss her cheek before she started the engine and pulled out onto the highway.

Within an hour, the two women arrived at the house in Chaffee that Molly and Jake bought years ago. "Your dad and I signed papers for this house on our second wedding anniversary," Molly sighed. "We were so happy then." Her voice trailed off.

They emerged from the cab of the pick-up just as the movers arrived. Entering the domain, Maggie smiled to see her earlier arrangements had been met.

The moving company packed everything in neat boxes, labeled and stacked in the living room. Together, mother and daughter went from box to box, and pointed out which ones would be going to Randolph with Molly. The rest would be picked up by Salvation Army in the morning. Following the boxes, they did the same with the furniture. The head-mover marked each item to be moved and assured Maggie everything would arrive in Massachusetts by 3:00 PM the next afternoon.

On their way out of town, they stopped by the real estate office. Maggie ran in to give them the key. Maggie had been unable to sell the house as planned. However, she finally came up with a satisfactory solution: She had spoken with the representative and arranged all the details about selling the house to the realtor who would then sell it in the open market.

The receptionist was a young woman with a warm smile. She immediately called Mr. Ellsworthy, who was to represent Maggie. When he arrived, Mags introduced herself, handed him the key, signed the papers he had brought, thanked him, and headed on her way.

Maggie was anxious to get all the business behind her and head south.

Mother and daughter talked of happy times, pleasant memories and future dreams as they headed for Massachusetts. Both women felt as if the past was truly behind them now. They could move on.

By the following week, Molly was well on her way to being settled in to her apartment. The workers had done an excellent job renovating her side of the duplex into a lovely one bedroom apartment. They had knocked out walls and built new ones in order to make the second bedroom part of Jeff and Maggie's house. The architect Jeff had hired worked closely with the laborers.Maggie, Jeff, and Molly were quite satisfied with the arrangements.

In a very short time, Molly and her granddaughter had become fast friends. Most importantly for Maggie she and Molly were truly becoming friends and deepening their relationship as mother and daughter.

Jeff had given Molly a job at his school. He hired her to be the head of his cafeteria staff. She was to plan all the menus, decor, and whatever else was needed to make meal time feel like home for the students. She loved the job and made it a point to talk to the kids each day. With Maggie's help as well as the students, Molly was becoming quite competent at signing.

Molly came over for supper the third Sunday in June. The day was special, because it marked the end of her second week in her new home. The day was special in another way also: It was Maggie's twenty-fifth birthday.

When Mags blew out her candles in the presence of her loving husband, adorable daughter, and special mother, she knew all her wishes had come true. Margaret Elizabeth Stelson Reyfield had finally found the pure happiness and love that she had longed for all her life.